How to Open a Restaurant:
DUE DILIGENCE

How to Open a Restaurant:
DUE DILIGENCE

*A Practical Guide and Workbook for
Realizing Your Vision with Confidence*

By Frank Stocco
Foodservice Consultant/Designer

nRD
Publishing

How to Open a Restaurant: Due Diligence

A project from National Restaurant Design, Inc.
http://www.NationalRD.com

Library of Congress Control Number: 2011920713
ISBN: 0-615-43969-1
ISBN: 978-0-615-43969-3

Cover design: Debbi Stocco
Photos and illustrations: Frank Stocco; Hannah Cooperrider; Debbi Stocco; Grand Restaurant Equipment and Design Company
Book design and typesetting: Debbi Stocco
Editing and proofreading: Sharon M. Knudson

NRD Publishing
books@nationalrd.com

Disclaimer: The purchaser of this publication assumes full responsibility for the use and interpretation of this material and information. The information in this book does not constitute legal advice. The publisher and author assume no liability whatsoever on behalf of the reader of this material. This book is not a substitute for consulting other professional services. Please consult with a lawyer and accountant to review laws, legal documents, leases, agreements and filings.

Printed in the United States of America

To my wife, Deborah
who worked harder
on this book than anyone.

Acknowledgements and Thanks

To my Mom and Dad, who taught me early on that intellect without hard work, dedication and perseverance is wasteful.

To The Culinary Institute of America in Hyde Park, New York, for an incredible education (class of 1975) that prepared me to succeed in this wonderful industry on many different levels.

To Bill Mandell, who was a mentor to me from the time I started working at age 15 and without whom the Culinary Institute would have remained just a dream.

To Chuck Otte, who inspired me to enter the design field.

To all of my colleagues in the foodservice industry. Each day was a new adventure, challenge and learning experience. I am thankful to all for letting me be a part of it!

Table of Contents

Foreword

There has never been a book in the foodservice industry that focuses solely on the expertise needed to *open* a restaurant. All the published books and manuals focus on restaurant and foodservice *management*. This manual is designed to provide a sort of "internship", preparing you thoroughly with a detailed guide to *opening* your restaurant within a required and realistic pre-opening budget. Visualizing and preparing such things as your concept and vision will save countless thousands of dollars in every aspect of opening, and ultimately operating your foodservice facility.

Preparation is key. There are statistics available that indicate the success and failure rate of foodservice facilities. These statistics do not tell you why restaurants fail, only that an unacceptable number do fail. So what does the general public and banking institution assume? They assume that restaurant failure is due to mismanagement and a lack of expertise. In some cases that is true. However, in most cases, the fate is sealed the day the restaurateur is fully committed to open a restaurant or foodservice facility.

The first question a venture capitalist or lending institution will ask you is, "What is your culinary background and are you qualified to *manage* a restaurant?" I am sure your answer will be a resounding "yes" and I am sure you will be able to back that up with documentation of exceptional qualifications. My question is, "Are you qualified to *open* a restaurant?" There are many great chefs and restaurant managers who have failed due to what happens before the restaurant opens. Was the restaurant mismanaged? Absolutely not. Think about it. Have you ever seen a restaurant close and wonder why because it was always so busy? It happens too much of the time.

The main reason so many restaurants fail is that they are mismanaged before, not after, they open. Most likely they were under-capitalized—even tens of thousands of dollars in the red, the day they opened. It is a very complex endeavor, but definitely not impossible. You can re-alize your vision with confidence if you do your "Due Diligence". In this step by step manual, *How to Open a Restaurant: Due Diligence,* I will take you from the conceptual stage to the Grand Opening so you can go beyond.

The goal is to save you literally thousands of dollars, and even help you gain financial acvan-tage by using this chronological comprehensive guide. Each instructional chapter is a work-book style manual with space for notes and vital information that pertains to the respective Instruction. Look at it as your internship.

Even seasoned restaurateurs will benefit from all of the tips, tactics and organizational information presented. When the 13 Instructions are studied and followed, the worksheets completed and your restaurant is open, you will have an in-depth journal that contains all of your critical information. This will serve as an invaluable resource for your success in future endeavors.

—Frank Stocco

Introduction

Opportunities in the foodservice industry are abundant. The foodservice industry and its interrelated commerce provide the largest base for employment in the world. It is also an industry without prejudice. Your gender, race, educational, religious or economic background do not matter. I have witnessed success from all segments of society. Your success will be determined by your ability to create and implement your vision. The following chapters compile a guide and an Instruction Manual for opening your foodservice facility. Whether you are creating a coffee shop, corporate cafeteria or full service restaurant, the same principles apply. To make things simple I will use the word "restaurant" to apply to all foodservice venues.

To start with, consider your qualifications. They must be diverse, as in the following list.

- **Passion**
  The difference between a great chef and a good chef is not knowledge or skill, it is the ability to unconditionally love and care for their art. Their greatest pleasure comes from delighting his or her patrons. All successful restaurants should have the same goal in mind—providing pleasure to the client. That can only be achieved with passion. Passionate restaurateurs find a way to make each aspect of the customer and employee experience wonderful.

- **Organization**
  Owning a restaurant is very similar to directing a movie. There are different teams of

people doing their part to make the production perfect. The ability to organize each team to perform their tasks in a flawless manner will create the best possible experience for the client.

- **Business**

  Having an understanding of income and cost analysis as well as expense categories and their relationship to income are paramount to success. The ability to analyze and micromanage your income will have a profound effect on your employees as well as your customers' experience.

- **Foodservice Knowledge**

  Using the analogy of a movie director again, he does not act, film or create the score for the movie, but I guarantee you that he or she has detailed knowledge of how each element creates the whole. While most great restaurant owners do not have culinary experience, they know how to surround themselves with people who will create that great steak, mix the perfect martini, and assemble a team of designers and professionals to achieve a wonderful customer experience.

Having acknowledged the necessary qualifications for *owning* a foodservice facility, this book in no way broaches the subject of *managing* a restaurant or foodservice facility. Quite truthfully, when you have the right qualifications, managing the restaurant is the easy part. The hard part is opening the restaurant. Most of what happens in the beginning stages of opening a restaurant has nothing to do with your ability to run a restaurant. Mistakes cannot be accepted in the developmental stages of opening a restaurant. For instance, if a bad meal is served or a drink is spilled, you will have an unhappy customer until your wit, charm and generosity can repair the customer's experience. It's not the end of the world. On the other hand, if you make a mistake in the developmental stage, it could cost you thousands of dollars and may even be as severe as not being able to open your restaurant. A mistake can cost you the art work for your walls, that great audio/visual system for your sports bar, or maybe the pre-opening operating cash needed to train your staff. In a word, the results can be "catastrophic." As you may have noticed, there are a large percentage of restaurants that close quickly after opening, and it's almost always due to having insufficient operating capital. If your full vision is not achieved, the customer experience suffers greatly. Your pre-opening budget can remain intact only if you do your due diligence.

The following chapters are an organizational guide for each developmental stage of opening a restaurant. Topics include, among others, Business Plan Development, Pre-Opening Budgeting, Permits, Financing, City, Fire and Health Department Regulations, ADA Requirements,

Leasing, and all aspects of Design, General Contracting and Purchasing. Each category is a task that requires flawless completion prior to opening. Each task is shown chronologically and each topic area features a checklist with space for your notes and contact information. The checklists not only help you focus on the tasks at hand in a step by step style, but help you delegate some of the tasks to others.

This is such a great industry—it's fun, exciting and profitable! Yet there is no money to waste. My hope is that you will read this manual from cover to cover, do your due diligence with knowledge, care and integrity, and then experience great success as a restaurateur. Nothing would make me happier than to be a small part of your accomplishment.

Instruction 1: *Concept and Vision*

Instruction 1: *Concept and Vision*

Concept
1: a scheme; a plan. 2: a central or unifying idea or theme.

Vision
1: force or power of imagination. 2: the ability to perceive some thing not actually visible, as through mental acuteness or keen foresight.

What is your restaurant "concept?" What is the "vision" for your site? These are two extraordinarily important questions, and one is much easier to answer than the other. To be sure, the question of vision is a bit harder to wrap your mind around. And why is this Instruction 1? It is fundamental. Instructions 2 through 13 will be completely irrelevant if you don't first understand your concept and vision. These become very personal, and you must reach absolute clarity early on. Go to 25 different restaurants and you will see some commonality, but you will also see each one's uniqueness. The menus will be different, the style of service, design, size of the space, artwork, furniture, smell, sound, décor and hundreds of other features that make the restaurant distinctively its own individual initiative. Key personnel, architects, designers and advisors will all require your succinct concept and vision. For this reason, I highly recommend including the name of the restaurant in your vision statement. While this is certainly optional, it will enhance and clarify your vision for everyone involved.

Instruction 1, Concept and Vision, is going to be the focus of your Business Plan in Instruction 2. Prospective investors and financial institutions will gauge much of their decision-making process on this. Your thesis has to play out like a movie in order for them to understand and get excited about your proposition. Sales projections are based on your past history, or if you are new to the business, on a hypothetical projection. Ask any novelist, screen writer or artist, and they'll tell you they start a project venture only after they have come to a very clear understanding of their concept and vision.

This is really the fun part of becoming a restaurateur—truly making your space your own—an expression of you. I could say more about the importance of Instruction 1, but that would be redundant. Let's get to it.

Concept

Concept is the nuts and bolts of your operation. Not only does it identify a theme, like fast food or white-table cloth (fine dining), it is a complete understanding and description of how your restaurant will function. The menu, style of service, seating capacity, price point, location, demographics and other distinctive features are included in your concept. The description does not need to be long, it needs to be clear and concise. There are countless concepts, and each one is unique to the person or group who created it. Each concept has a two- or three-word description, such as Brew Pub, Sports Bar, California Fusion, Bakery Café, New York Deli, Gastro Pub, Japanese Steak House, Chop House, Wine Bar, Pizzeria, etc.

The following table is an example of what should be included in identifying your concept. Fill in words and descriptions on the next few pages that are associated with your concept.

Sample Concept Features and Description	
Feature	**Sample Concept**
Name	Ruben's Gourmet Deli
Description	New York Deli
Service	Fast casual with large volume take-out and catering
Menu	Gourmet sandwiches, fresh soups, salads, beer, wine, espresso, gourmet cheesecakes
Price Point	$10.00 to $12.00
Key Staff	Chef Leonard Ruben
Site	Medium to large city, dense white-collar demographics, high-volume foot and car traffic
Space (sq. ft.)	2,000 to 3,000
Seating	75-100
Atmosphere	High energy, fun

Sample Concept Description:

Ruben's Gourmet Deli is an upscale, casual eatery. The focus is on fresh, oversized sandwiches, salads, soups and several flavors of New York style cheesecakes along with a great beer and wine selection. Sandwiches will be made with the finest meats, such as Carnegie Corned Beef and Pastrami on homemade Jewish rye, cut thin and stacked high. Salads and soups will be made daily with the finest ingredients possible. Chef Ruben's award-winning cheesecake will complete the dining experience. Our perfect store size is

2,800 square feet. The space will allow seating for approximately 80 patrons, and have a kitchen and display area large enough to produce a quality product with a big focus on high-volume catering and take-out. The perfect location is a white collar business district with high traffic. Other restaurants and retail stores in the area will be imperative to success. The customer experience will be that of a fun, high-energy establishment. The customer will walk in through the main entrance and immediately be directed to the counter, where they will be greeted by cashiers. Adjacent to the cashiers will be a bakery case loaded with cheesecakes that entice the customer to have a slice with their meal or take a slice to go. The customer will order their meal and beverage from large menu boards near the cashier, and then follow a line where they can see the staff slice their meat, assemble their sandwich and salad, and pour the soup to finish their meal. They will then be seated. The service is fast, allowing a business person to enjoy a great meal in 20 to 45 minutes for around $12. The style of service will create an enormous amount of energy. The banter between the customers and the staff will be part of the meal assembly process. The concept also reduces labor costs by requiring minimal waitstaff.

The above example gives you an idea of a concept description. It touches on all the important points that make up a foodservice establishment. You may want to be more detailed in certain areas when you formulate your own concept. For example, you might want to talk more about your chef—he/she may be high profile and can attract business by name recognition. Maybe all the food will be prepared with local organic products, or perhaps there is something else deserving of special mention.

Use the following worksheet to describe and identify the features of your own concept. You will need this in order to complete your Business Plan in the next chapter.

Your Concept Features and Description	
Feature	*Your Concept*
Name	
Description	
Service	
Menu	
Price Point	
Key Staff	
Site	
Space (sq. ft.)	
Seating	
Atmosphere	

Concept Description:

_____
_____
_____
_____
_____
_____
_____
_____
_____
_____
_____
_____
_____
_____
_____
_____
_____
_____
_____
_____
_____
_____
_____
_____
_____
_____
_____
_____
_____
_____
_____
_____
_____
_____
_____

Vision

The topic of vision is definitely more abstract. I always apply a sensory theory to all restaurants that we help design and develop. Using the five senses of sight, hearing, taste, smell and touch will clarify your vision. Let's take each sense and examine how it relates to your restaurant.

Sight—what your place looks like such as walls, flooring, ceiling, cabinetry, seating, artwork, signage, televisions, employee uniforms, plate and glassware and many other items that will create the look that you require.

Hearing—is your restaurant going to be loud and exciting or subdued and mellow? This sense will help you discover the ambiance.

Taste—this is a description of your flavors. Describe this with terms like fruitful, big bold flavors, delicate to the pallet, pungent, spicy and bitter—words that can help identify the style of food on your menu. Your description should make the person reading this hungry for your fare.

Smell—this a bit tougher to describe. You may want to say, "The smell of fresh baked breads will instantly remind you of the great care we take to make all of our food fresh and wholesome." If you are a brew pub you would want to describe the aroma of the brewing hops. A simple one or two line description of smell will greatly add to your narrative.

Touch—the human body will come into contact with hundreds of items in your restaurant such as tables, chairs, menus, food, restrooms, silverware, glassware, coffee mugs, etc. A booth package can be manufactured for 20 different concepts. If you are a steakhouse with wood floors, stone walls and a large fireplace you may want soft upholstered booths. If you are a 50's dinner you will want hard bright surfaces.

Every great restaurant and restaurant designer will incorporate all of these sensory elements into the design. Can you imagine a restaurant with no art or sound? You want your customers to have the best possible experience. Pay close attention to all. Answer all of the sensory questions and I guarantee that you will have a well branded vision.

Please write out your vision on the next page. This will be needed to complete your Business Plan.

Vision:

_____
_____
_____
_____
_____
_____
_____
_____
_____
_____
_____
_____
_____
_____
_____
_____
_____
_____
_____
_____
_____
_____
_____
_____
_____
_____
_____
_____
_____
_____
_____
_____
_____
_____
_____

Concept and Vision

Now is the time to meld concept and vision together to create the description for your exciting new restaurant. The exercises you have completed will enable you to write a great Business Plan, attract investors, and hire key personnel, architects, a foodservice designer, and an interior designer. Their understanding of your concept and vision will reduce mistakes and save you thousands of dollars. You now have a great understanding of how your space is to look, feel and operate.

Write an essay description of your restaurant. If you need more space you can write it out in another notebook. This description will be applied to the Foreword of your Business Plan.

Concept and Vision:

_____
_____
_____
_____
_____
_____
_____
_____
_____
_____
_____
_____
_____
_____
_____
_____
_____
_____
_____
_____
_____
_____
_____
_____
_____
_____

_____
_____
_____
_____
_____
_____
_____
_____
_____
_____
_____
_____
_____
_____
_____
_____

Restaurant Name

Now that you have identified your Concept and Vision you will want to register the name of your restaurant. Registering your name is very inexpensive. Search with the Secretary of State on the State Web site to see if it is already registered and in use. Complete the checklist in this Instruction before moving to Instruction 2.

Checklist	Complete	N/A	Notes
Business Name			
Concept			
Vision			
Concept/Vision Essay			
Register Name			
Other			

Notes

Instruction 2: *Business Plan*

Instruction 2: *Business Plan*

> "The best business plans are straight-forward documents that
> spell out the who, what, where, why, and how much..."
>
> — PAULA NELSON, ENTREPRENEUR AND BEST SELLING AUTHOR

Business Plans are assembled for two primary reasons. The first is for gathering all the information necessary to have an educated and rational discussion on the feasibility of opening your restaurant. The second is to attract prospective investors if financing becomes necessary. Most Business Plans are based on hypothetical information, and this is especially true for first time entrepreneurs. I am a big believer in putting together a Business Plan that is 100% accurate, with full disclosure. It's not complicated but does require some research. What if your Business Plan is inaccurate, or you fail to get actual estimates on equipment, ventilation and contracting costs? Poor planning can be catastrophic, and your mistakes could cost you thousands of dollars. A great Business Plan that has accurate data can help you form a highly educated analysis, and frankly, is the only way to attract funding. Be honest with yourself, and don't tell people "what they want to hear"—tell them the truth. Don't start a project with inaccurate data or you'll get half way through the project and discover you're $50,000 under funded. Due diligence is the operative phrase, so save yourself real pain by working hard to obtain thorough information, first.

There are many companies that write great Business Plans for a living. There are also professional consultants that will put together an entire Business Plan or help you write your own, but they will be extremely expensive. Or you can buy a relatively inexpensive computer program that will organize your information and make your plan extremely presentable. In any case, all three options require that you gather the pertinent information. The larger and more complicated your restaurant, the more you will need assistance in putting together a great plan. Following is a listing of the categories for which you will need to gather vital information. I have also included some optional categories that will enhance your plan. Some of these can cost extra money but you might consider it money well spent.

A comprehensive Restaurant Business Plan is made up of nine main categories of information, and each grouping has subcategories as defined below.

Business Plan Categories

1. Introduction

- **Concept and Vision**

  Begin with this section and make it count. If prospective investors love your vision, they will be very intrigued and continue to read the rest of your Business Plan.

- **Directors**

  Name the players in your plan. Who has ownership?

- **Management Team**

  This is a list of all your key employees. For example, in a large restaurant there will be a Food and Beverage Director, Executive Chef, Dining Room Manager, Bar Manager, Wine Steward, and possibly even a Financial Controller.

- **Business Philosophy**

  What is your approach or philosophy for operating a successful restaurant? Can your management style create a great atmosphere for employees as well as a wonderful experience for customers?

- **Geographical Strategy**

  Tell why your proposed location is the most advantageous for the success of your restaurant concept. It might have high foot traffic, be next to a large retail anchor, have a high income demographic, be in a college town, etc.

- **Vision for the Future**

  Most potential investors want to see a major upside for their investment. Be honest about your future plans. If you are anticipating additional restaurant locations in the future, create a time table for those. Investors like the assurance that they will be a part of future growth endeavors.

- **Competition**

  Gather sales information and data on similar concepts with similar demographics. This information will help investors understand that with your expertise, the concept should outperform like-competition. List a few establishments and their revenues. This will give your investors a good comfort level about the feasibility of your concept.

- **Art and Design** (optional)

  I highly recommend that you include some branding ideas and visuals. These two important elements illustrate your vision. First, you will need logos, artistic interior renderings, and sign art. These visuals will help take your concept and vision to a "branded" state. A good graphic designer/architect can depict your vision professionally so your investors will be able to picture your concept and vision. Secondly, you will need a concept drawing of the restaurant layout. I highly recommend that you engage a foodservice designer to create a concept drawing that demonstrates to investors and key personnel the functionality of the concept—how it flows, operates and services the customer. The concept drawing will also show all of the equipment and components of an operating restaurant, and that's its biggest attribute. Using a concept drawing, you can get accurate pricing from equipment dealers and contractors. This makes your pre-opening budget very accurate, and investors will be impressed with your meticulous attention to detail. Concept drawings not only legitimize the project for your investors, but will give you a comfort level that can only be attained by putting together a budget based on detailed drawings. I highly recommend them, especially if your project exceeds $100,000. Spend the money. The few thousand dollars you spend now will save you $20,000 or more later.

2. Organizational Structure

- **Management and Personnel**

  Identify your key personnel with a brief history of each one's expertise. These are the non-management employees needed to operate your facility. How many cooks, waitstaff and other categories of staff are essential for a proper, smooth operation? If yours is a large restaurant, you will want to include the Food and Beverage Director, Executive Chef, General Manager, Wine Steward, Controller and Dining Room Manager. If you are opening a coffee shop, you might need just an experienced Manager and Barista. This is an important exercise to do, and the information will be a key component to your sales, labor and cost projections.

- **Administrative Organization**

  How are you going to achieve profitability? Someone in your organization will ultimately be responsible for profit and loss. This person must have an understanding of food, labor and fixed cost controls. You will also need to decide if you're going to have a Human Resource department. Regardless of the size of your organization, you need to develop employee manuals. While small foodservice venues will most likely be the sole responsibility of the owner, larger institutions will have several administrative personnel. Describe the executive chain of command and some of their responsibilities. Your investors will want to know who is navigating the ship.

3. Restaurant Operations

- **Structure of the Building**

  Even if you are in the early stages and have not yet selected a site for your restaurant, describe in detail the optimal building required for your concept. Include information such as the size, architectural features, whether it will be free standing or in a strip mall, if the space requires an end-cap for a drive-thru window, if the space needs to be wide for maximum visibility, etc.

- **Location**

  What is the best location for your restaurant? List the reasons why one site is better than another. Your location should always be based on profitability, not sales, so describe the types of locations that will best assure profitability. If you have already selected a specific site, take photographs and include all the pertinent site information in your Business Plan. Prime locations may cost $60.00 per square foot, and that might be a good idea if you can generate the volume needed in order to be extremely profitable. However, there is a danger in putting a specific location in the Business Plan. Your first mission is to sell your investors on an idea, and sometimes too much information can cloud this process. You be the judge.

- **Layout Drawing** (optional)

  I touched on this subject when I introduced the concept of a Business Plan. A detailed layout drawing of your restaurant is a great tool for understanding concept, vision, flow, costs, and the structure itself. Do your due diligence. Although I say the restaurant layout is optional, the money spent will be well worth it to you and your investors. There's nothing quite like a visual graphic depiction of your idea to bring clarity.

4. Marketing

- **Product Mix**

  Describe your menu by giving a detailed outline of your food and beverage service. A description of your product mix creates an understanding of your food and beverage focus. If you are a steak house that also sells seafood, articulate that. If you are a restaurant with a $100,000 wine inventory, give a narrative that portrays the pairings of food and wine. Don't include your full menu—it will just clutter your Business Plan. If you have already constructed one, include it in a separate marketing package.

- **Sales Estimates**

  Explain your anticipated sales. Consider things like-competition, location and demographics. This is not a profit and loss analysis.

- **The Competition**

  What is your competition doing that makes them successful and profitable? What are their sales? What advertising tactics do they employ to attract customers? Name other restaurants that your investors are familiar with as comparisons. Assure your investors that your marketing strategies and operating skills will best your competition, but make sure that any information you provide is accurate.

- **Market Analysis**

  Describe your clientele, population, street traffic, medium income, foot traffic, and retail anchors, as well as major draws such as stadiums, colleges, office complexes, a train station, hospitals, and any other nearby institutions that are beneficial to your business. Do your research. You must be 100% sure that your location of choice is your best opportunity for high volume sales and profits. You do not want to mislead your potential investors, nor yourself.

- **Marketing and Advertising**

  This is your strategy for attracting customers. Indicate the percentage of sales you will dedicate to marketing. Also show the best sources for advertising and promotion that best suit your concept. If you are a pizzeria, for example, you will want to focus on coupon and direct mail programs. In some cities you can't sell a pizza without a coupon. If you are a sports bar, you will want to devise an advertising plan that includes radio stations, local team sponsorship, and newspaper ads. If you have a good plan, it shows you will work hard to find ways to increase sales. Good food alone will not be enough.

- **Pricing Policy**

  Many factors go into creating a pricing policy: the cost of occupancy, food, labor, beverage, competition, demographics, and fixed costs. Your pricing should not necessarily be more or less than your competitor's. Describe your approach to pricing—more than likely you will be similar to your competition. If there is a steak house in the vicinity that is selling a fillet for $15 and you plan on charging $25, you must be able to justify your strategy to the investors and your customers. Your goal is to give value based on food, service and ambience.

5. Historic Analysis

This category shows a history and is based on your existing restaurant or a prior one, as long as it is the same concept as your new, proposed restaurant. If this concept is new for you, you'll have to do research on existing restaurants with like-concepts.

- **General View**

  What is the national or educated view of your concept? Has it run its course? This often happens with theme restaurants—they're fun for a while but overstay their welcome. In the late 1990s, for example, cigar and martini lounges were the big craze. Today you'll have a hard time finding one because of the smoking bans. Make sure you have a concept that is sound and ready for the long haul. Write a short essay on the history of your concept. Do not be afraid to romanticize this a bit—it's an extension of your vision.

- **The Market Position**

  Market position has everything to do with the community you are in. If you are in New York City, you can open a Sushi Bar, or for that matter, any conceivable concept imaginable. There are millions of people in New York City from whom to get business. But a small town like Gillette, Wyoming is an entirely different matter. If you are opening a Sushi Bar there, be sure of your market position. Always gather sound information to validate your concept in relation to the location, and make sure there is a market in the area you are considering.

- **Past Income Statement**

  If you have previously owned a restaurant or a business, include an income statement in your Business Plan that illustrates your ability to manage income successfully. If this is your first venue, I would ask that you not include this category. We will cover financial projections a bit later.

- **Past Balance Sheet**

  If you have previously owned a restaurant or business, include a balance sheet in your Business Plan. It will illustrate your ability to successfully manage profit and loss. Don't include this category if this is your first venue. Again, we will cover financial projections later on.

6. Financial Plan

- **Investment Budget**

  This is a compilation of the necessary monies needed for opening your restaurant with an operating cash reserve. You will need to do a lot of research for this. The only accurate way to achieve a pre-opening budget is to investigate and project the cost of every possible aspect. You will have to engage architects, designers, contractors, agencies, landlords, and several equipment and furniture dealers. I urge you to have your concept drawing in hand to help you achieve the most accurate projections—otherwise you may attract investors, but it's possible they can only afford what you project and request, leaving you short of the actual need. It comes down to the due diligence.

- **Cost Projections**

  Investigate and then check off the following list of cost projections.

  ❏ All construction costs including carpentry, plumbing, electrical and HVAC

  ❏ Permits

  ❏ Licensing

- ❏ Insurance legal work, employee manuals and literature
- ❏ Designers
- ❏ Accounting
- ❏ Computers and P.O.S. systems
- ❏ Kitchen and bar equipment
- ❏ Furniture
- ❏ Utilities
- ❏ Office equipment
- ❏ Audio/Visual
- ❏ Smallwares
- ❏ Table top items
- ❏ Printing
- ❏ Marketing and advertising
- ❏ Services: phone, data, linen, garbage, water, gas and electricity
- ❏ Pre-opening employment of key personnel
- ❏ Employee training
- ❏ All inventories
- ❏ Operating capital
- ❏ Overruns and miscellaneous

The above list shows general categories, but there may be other costs associated with your particular concept as well. For example, part of your concept might include a bowling alley or video games. Just keep in mind that all the costs associated with your pre-opening budget should be included in the Business Plan. Be precise and truthful with full transparency. An accurate design drawing will be invaluable for acquiring pricing and minimizing unforeseen expenses and surcharges. Without a design, an equipment supplier, contractor, electrician, plumber, or HVAC contractor may not even want to get involved in the project. If they lack information on which to base pricing, they won't want to spend the necessary time to bid on your project. Once you have the bids for establishing your budget, add 10% to each line item. These subjects will be covered again later.

- **Income to Cost Ratio**
  This ratio is the relationship of costs to total sales. If your sales for the month is $100,000 and the cost of food is $30,000, your food cost ratio/percentage is food cost ÷ sales, or 30%. Every cost category will have an associated ratio/percentage.

- **Return on Investment (ROI)**

  ROI is your net annual return divided by the investment. The return on investment is most often stated as an annualized rate of return, and is most often given for a calendar or fiscal year. It is used to compare returns on investments with money gained or lost. If your net annual return is $20,000 and the investment is $100,000, your ROI is 20%: $20,000 ÷ $100,000 = 20% ROI. This is a key component for raising investor interest and money, if needed. You must indicate the investor ownership/profit percentage in your Business Plan so using a sales model, the investor will understand their ROI. Your Business Plan must include a concise illustration of an ROI formula. For example, you have a total investment of $500,000, the sales in your first year are $1,000,000, and your net profit from the sales is $150,000 for a 15% net profit. Your first year's return on investment/ROI is 30% (net profit $150,000 ÷ investment $500,000 = an ROI of 30%). The same scenario with the addition of a $50,000 investor who has negotiated with you a 10% ownership stake would have the same ROI: $150,000 x 10% = $15,000 = an ROI of 30%, which is the same. Raising funds is always a challenge. If your concept, vision and Business Plan is fundamentally sound, you will have a solid ROI model and an easy time attracting investors. The restaurant industry has a reputation for being risky so a 30% ROI is a good number to aim for. If you have a need to recruit investors, make sure there is a big up-side—risk versus reward. ROI equations will also be included in your profit and loss projections. The subject of ROI will be revisited in the next Instruction on financing.

- **Sales and Cost Projections**

  There are industry models that can help a first-time restaurant owner arrive at profitable ratios, but be aware that each concept will have slightly different ratios. For example, a breakfast style restaurant will have a lower food cost than a steak house but that doesn't mean one is better than another. If you are selling an omelet for $6 that costs $2 to produce, you have a 33% food cost and $4 gross profit. If you are selling a steak for $20 and it costs $10 to produce, you have a 50% food cost and $10 gross profit. The steak has a higher gross profit with a higher food cost percentage. Which gross profit would you choose? This illustration shows that lower food costs do not always translate into big profits. That being said, cost percentages are the only way to control profit and loss. If you're going to micro-manage any aspect of your operation, it should be your income to cost ratio. With constant analysis, quick adjustments can be made. For the purpose of your Business Plan, you must find out what a typical cost to sales percentage is for every category of your concept's costs. The truth is that a breakfast restaurant's food cost will not vary much from that of a steak house. See the sample profit and loss statement on page 38. The percentages indicated are those of a typical restaurant, and you will see a cost percentage associated with each cost category. In order to achieve profitability, your cost percentages will need to be controlled. If your food cost is 33%, labor is 28%, rent is 7%, utilities are 2%, advertising is 3%, and your sewer, water and other services are 2%, there is not much left over. In order to assure profitability, all categories need to be ruthlessly micro-managed. Use the provided example and modify it for your concept. If you have arcade or display sales, make sure they are part of the cost-to-sales ratio. Remember, your sales and costs projection is your financial model and will show in detail how financially viable your concept is. Can you make a go of it? Will a lending institution or investors want to participate? Make sure every bit of information can be backed up with statistical data. Lending institutions and investors will ask questions concerning each line item so be ready to have your Business Plan scrutinized and questioned.

- **Financial Revenue and Cost Synopsis**
  This is your financial model. Your Business Plan projections should be shown using four columns:

  1. **Break-Even**
     What is the least amount of sales that will result in a financial break-even? All of your cost percentages will change with the exception of your cost of goods sold. Food and liquor percentages can be controlled, but labor costs will be elevated because you still have to staff the restaurant. It is always harder to control labor costs when you have lower than anticipated sales.

  2. **Year One Projection**
     Your sales projections can be aggressive, but your cost of doing business will always be higher the first year. Labor will be higher because of training, turnover and over-staffing due to inexperienced employees. For that reason, consider projecting a 3% above normal labor cost. Food and liquor will also be elevated by 3% because of all the training, waste, research and development, and grand opening give-a-ways. All other categories will stay constant. Even if your expectations may be for a 15% profit, project your first year's sales at least 6% lower than that. Keep in mind that any savvy investor will understand and appreciate your candor. Full profitability in the first year is virtually unattainable.

  3. **Year Two Projection**
     Adjust your sales up 10% to 20%. If your business model suggested that your profit would be 15%, show it for your second year's profit. The rational for this is two-fold. First, you will want to implement yearly price increases—it's reasonable to raise prices every year, and for some concepts, every month. Second, anticipate an increasing customer base.

  4. **Year Three Projection**
     Use the same principles for Year Two with the exception of your profit margin. Fixed costs like insurance, waste, rent, telephone, cable TV, etc. will remain fairly constant, and this will elevate the net profit by a point or two. Always increase every category cost, but if you know, for example, that your insurance cost was $5,000 in the prior year and will remain the same this year, your percentage of cost to sales may be a ¼% less. It all adds up to a possible 1or 2% increase in net profits.

Explain in a few sentences your justification for each year's projections, including your break-even projection. Remember to add in cost categories that may be exclusive to your concept. See a sample Financial Business Model on the next page. The percentages used are industry norms, but the percentages will vary by concept and geographical location. Below is a cost category list with basic explanations.

- ❏ Lunch Sales—food sales for lunch.
- ❏ Dinner Sales—food sales for dinner.
- ❏ Liquor Sales—total day's liquor sales.
- ❏ Total Sales—total day's food and liquor sales = 100%.
- ❏ Food and Beverage Costs—total cost of food. Formula: food and beverage cost ÷ food and beverage sales = %.
- ❏ Liquor Costs—total cost of liquor. Formula: liquor cost ÷ liquor sales = %.
- ❏ Cost of Goods Sold—liquor and food cost ÷ total food, beverage and liquor sales = %.
- ❏ Operating Expense—cost of doing business minus food, beverage and liquor sales.
- ❏ Advertising—all forms of advertising: newspaper ads, yellow pages, commercials, flyers, advertising art, etc.
- ❏ Automobile—company car.
- ❏ Bad Debt—bad checks, walk-outs, uncollected sales of any kind.
- ❏ Bank Charges—the cost of banking, checks.
- ❏ Credit Card Fees—credit card company fees.
- ❏ Depreciation—a fund that allows you to replace equipment.
- ❏ Dues and Subscriptions—newspapers, institutional magazines, clubs, etc.
- ❏ Equipment Leasing—all foodservice equipment that is leased.
- ❏ Insurance, General—liability, fire, theft.
- ❏ Insurance, Workman's Comp.—required insurance for employee accidents.
- ❏ Insurance, Health—cost of health insurance benefit for qualified employees.
- ❏ Insurance, Auto—company car insurance.
- ❏ Insurance Dram Shop—liquor liability.
- ❏ Licenses and Permits—food and liquor licenses, and any permits required.
- ❏ Office Expense—supplies and office equipment needs.
- ❏ Payroll—gross wages for all employees. Categories for managers, cooks, bartenders and waitstaff can be shown in separate columns but this is not necessary for the Business Plan.

- ❏ Payroll Taxes—employer contributions, Social Security, Medicare, unemployment insurance.
- ❏ Postage and Delivery—mailings, not including advertising.
- ❏ Printing and Reproduction—menus, placemats, bags, napkins, etc.
- ❏ Professional Fees—accountants, lawyers.
- ❏ Research and Development—checking out the competition, experimenting with new menu items, etc.
- ❏ Rent CAM—Common Area Maintenance: plowing, landscaping, building maintenance, parking lot up-keep. This charge is in addition to base rent. This category can be eliminated for building owners and reclassified as Outside Building and Grounds Maintenance.
- ❏ Rent—the cost of space. Building owners can reclassify this as Mortgage Cost.
- ❏ Repair and Maintenance—any repairs to equipment and the building.
- ❏ Supplies—paper goods, dishes, smallwares, detergent, and supplies.
- ❏ Telephone—telephone lines.
- ❏ Travel—travel expenses.
- ❏ Utilities and Services—gas, electric, waste, water, and cable. Additional categories can be added to separate items but are not necessary for the Business Plan.
- ❏ Web site and Internet—Internet access, Web site posting, maintenance fees.
- ❏ Total Expenses—the total of all food and liquor expenses. Total Expenses ÷ sales = %.
- ❏ Gross Profit—total sales minus the costs of food and liquor.
- ❏ Net Income—total sales minus cost of food, liquor and expenses = net income. Food, liquor and expenses÷sales=profit %.
- ❏ Total Investment—cost of opening plus operating capital.
- ❏ ROI—return on investment.

The columns you use for an actual Profit and Loss Statement will be further separated by categories. You will want to break down management costs by hourly labor costs. Gas, electric, waste, and linen should also become separate lines to help you micro-manage your costs.

Some lending institutions require month by month projections. Because this is a sales projection for a business model, I do not see the need unless your model is highly seasonal. Doing a month by month is always a good exercise, though, so do what is necessary for your situation.

Sample Financial Business Model —The Royal Fox Restaurant

Sales and Costs	Break Even	%	Year One	%	Year Two	%	Year Three	%
Lunch Sales Food	225,000.00	100	350,000.00	100	385,000.00	100	423,500.00	100
Dinner Sales Food	525,000.00	100	600,000.00	100	660,000.00	100	726,000.00	100
Liquor Sales	100,000.00	100	150,000.00	100	165,000.00	100	181,500.00	100.00
Total Sales	850,000.00	100	1,100,000.00	100	1,210,000.00	100	1,331,000.00	100
Operating Expenses								
Food & Bev. Costs	306,000.00	36	342,000.00	36	344,850.00	33	379,335.00	33
Liquor Costs	21,000.00	21	31,500.00	21	29,700.00	18	32,670.00	18
Cost of Goods Sold	327,000.00	38	373,500.00	34	374,550.00	31	412,005.00	31
Gross Profit	591,000.00	64	726,500.00	66	835,450.00	69	918,995.00	69
Operating Expense								
Advertising	22,000.00	2.5	22,000.00	2	24,200.00	2	26,620.00	2
Automobile	5,400.00	.3	5,400.00	0.3	5,400.00	0.3	6,000.00	.3
Bad Dept	1,000.00	.1	1,000.00	.1	1,200.00	.1	1,800.00	.1
Bank Charges	1,200.00	.1	1,200.00	.1	1,320.00	.1	1,500.00	.1
Credit Card Fees	9,400.00	1	11,500.00	1	14,120.00	1	18,965.00	1
Depreciation	6,000.00	.7	6,000.00	.5	6,000.00	.5	6,000.00	.5
Dues & Subscriptions	1,200.00	.1	1,200.00	.1	1,200.00	.1	1,400.00	.1
Equipment Leasing	2,160.00	.3	2,160.00	.25	2,160.00	.25	2,160.00	.25
Insurance – General	6,000.00	.7	6,000.00	.5	6,000.00	.5	6,300.00	.5
Insurance Workman	5,760.00	.7	6,600.00	.5	6,776.00	.5	6,950.00	.5
Insurance – Health	18,000.00	2	18,000.00	1.6	21,000.00	1.7	21,000.00	1.6
Insurance – Auto	2,700.00	.3	2,700.00	.25	2,900.00	.25	3,100.00	.25
Insurance- Dram Shop	6,000.00	.7	6,000.00	.5	6,600.00	.5	7,200.00	.5
Licenses and Permits	15,000.00	1.7	15,000.00	1.3	15,000.00	1.2	15,000.00	1.1
Office Expense	1,700.00	.2	1,800.00	.2	1,980.00	.2	2,150.00	.2
Payroll	297,000.00	35	330,000.00	30	338,800.00	28	366,800.00	28
Payroll Taxes	23,760.00	2.7	26,400.00	2.4	27,104.00	2.2	29,344.00	2.2
Postage and Delivery	300.00	.1	300.00	.1	330.00	.1	350.00	.1
Printing & Repro	750.00	.1	750.00	.1	950.00	.1	1,100.00	.1
Professional Fees	3,000.00	.4	3,000.00	.25	3,300.00	.25	3,500.00	.25
Research & Develop.	2,500.00	.3	2,500.00	.25	3,000.00	.25	3000.00	.25
Rent CAM	12,000.00	1.5	12,000.00	1	12,000.00	1	12,000.00	.9
Rent	54,000.00	6	54,000.00	5	56,700.00	4.6	59,535.00	4.5
Repair & Maint.	4,000.00	.5	4,000.00	.5	4,800.00	.5	6,000.00	.5
Supplies	9,000.00	1	11,000.00	1	14,100.00	1	15,300.00	1
Telephone	2,400.00	.3	2,400.00	.2	2,400.00	.2	2,500.00	.2
Travel	2,500.00	.3	2,500.00	.25	3,500.00	.25	4,000.00	.25
Utilities and Services	23,000.00	2.7	24,000.00	2	26,500.00	2	28,500.00	2
Website and Internet	1,200.00	.1	1,200.00	.1	1,200.00	.1	1,300.00	.1
Total Expenses	538,930.00	61	580,610.00	53	610,540.00	50	659,374.00	50
Gross Profit	541,000.00	64	726,500.00	66	835,450.00	69	918,995.00	69
Net Income	2,070.00	.2%	145,890.00	13%	224,910.00	19%	259,621.00	19%
Total Investment	600,000.00		600,000.00		600,000.00		600,000.00	
ROI		0%		24%		37%		43%

7. Risk Management

Do you have a business model that incorporates some fail-safe measures? This can take many forms. Maybe instead of a long-term lease, you could have a short-term lease with various options to renew. Do you have a buyout in your lease that will allow for an early departure? Are you using investor money instead of banking money? Are you signed personally for loans, leasing and consumables? Your business model should briefly explain how, if failure is unavoidable, you can reduce the risk.

- **Risk Management Strategy**—a rainy day fund, lease requirements, employee expense-cutting initiatives, and anything else that suggests you have done everything you can to reduce risk.

- **Exit Strategy**—What is your strategy for selling or liquidating in good times and bad? I would not give much attention to this inclusion because it could have a negative connotation if phrased poorly. Be sure this sounds positive so the lending institutions and investors will praise your attention to detail and conclude that you have the welfare of everyone associated with the project in mind.

8. Personal Information

Personal information consists of a short resume, information about your family, and a personal income and financial balance sheet. All investors and lending institutions require this information because they want to know the risk is spread out evenly. What do you have to lose? If your fraction of the deal is risk free, you will have a very hard time attracting investors.

9. Business Plan Closing Statement

The Closing Statement is a recap of your Business Plan. Reiterate your belief in your business model.

Business Plan Checklist and Worksheet

You are now ready to complete the worksheet and checklist on the following pages. You'll find a helpful checklist of the items and topics discussed. The quality of your Business Plan will make or break you, so be thorough and honest in your assumptions. As stated earlier, there are many computer programs for well under $100 that will help keep your plan organized and add attractive graphics. I highly recommend that you check out a few of these programs. There are also professional consultants that will prepare a plan for you, but this is an expensive way to proceed. With the information provided above, you should be able to write up a very comprehensive plan without the need of a consultant.

Business Plan Topic	Complete	N/A	Notes
1. Introduction			
Concept and Vision			
Directors			
Management Team			
Business Philosophy			
Geographical Strategy			
Vision for the Future			
Competition			
Art and Design			
2. Organizational Structure			
Management and Personnel			
Administrative Organization			
3. Restaurant Operations			
Structure of the Building			
Location			
Layout Drawing			
4. Marketing			
The Product Mix			
Sales Estimates			
The Competition			
Market Analysis			
Marketing and Advertising			
Pricing Policy			
5. Historic Analysis			
General View			
The Market Position			
Past Income Statement			
Past Balance Sheet			

Business Plan Topic	Complete	N/A	Notes
6. Financial Plan			
Investment Budget			
Cost Projections			
Income to Cost Ratio			
Return on Investment (ROI)			
Sales and Cost Projections			
Financial Revenue and Cost Synopsis			
1. Break Even Projection			
2. Year One Projection			
3. Year Two Projection			
4. Year Three Projection			
7. Risk Management			
Risk Management Strategy			
Exit Strategy			
8. Personal Information			
Resume			
Family Information			
Income and Financial Statement			
9. Closing Statement			
10. Other			

Contacts Pertinent to Business Plan	
Name: Company: Phone(s): E-mail: Other:	
Name: Company: Phone(s): E-mail: Other:	
Name: Company: Phone(s): E-mail: Other:	
Name: Company: Phone(s): E-mail: Other:	
Name: Company: Phone(s): E-mail: Other:	

Contacts Pertinent to Business Plan	
Name: Company: Phone(s): E-mail: Other:	
Name: Company: Phone(s): E-mail: Other:	
Name: Company: Phone(s): E-mail: Other:	
Name: Company: Phone(s): E-mail: Other:	
Name: Company: Phone(s): E-mail: Other:	

Contacts Pertinent to Business Plan	
Name: Company: Phone(s): E-mail: Other:	
Name: Company: Phone(s): E-mail: Other:	
Name: Company: Phone(s): E-mail: Other:	
Name: Company: Phone(s): E-mail: Other:	
Name: Company: Phone(s): E-mail: Other:	

Contacts Pertinent to Business Plan	
Name: Company: Phone(s): E-mail: Other:	
Name: Company: Phone(s): E-mail: Other:	
Name: Company: Phone(s): E-mail: Other:	
Name: Company: Phone(s): E-mail: Other:	
Name: Company: Phone(s): E-mail: Other:	

Instruction 3: *Financing*

Instruction 3: *Financing*

"Demonstrate confidence—like you have done this many times before. Be prepared to answer questions about every aspect of your plan with accuracy and intelligence."

— FRANK STOCCO, FOODSERVICE CONSULTANT

There are many ways to fund your restaurant project, and some forms of financing are more difficult than others. First-time restaurateurs often find it much more difficult to secure a loan than someone who has previously owned a restaurant or a business. Lending institutions and investors have one thing in common—they don't want bad debts on their record.

Whether you secure a loan or not will depend on your ability to convince lenders and investors that your project is low risk with high profits. How do you convince them? Have a great Business Plan. Make sure it is evident that in a worst case scenario, you have a great deal to lose personally. They want to know, for example, that you are investing some of your own cash. That, along with your personal professionalism, is key. That's the reason such a big emphasis was put on Instructions 1 and 2. The people who analyze your Business Plan are highly astute at scrutinizing business models—if there are any holes in your plan, they will recognize them and you will not get funded. Dress appropriately when going to an interview or a meeting. Be professional. Demonstrate confidence. Act like you have done this many times before. Be prepared to answer questions about every aspect of your plan with accuracy and intelligence.

You will see from the list on the following page that there are many ways to fund a restaurant. If there is real estate involved, there may be more than one loan in the package. Most lending institutions and investors like to separate the real estate from the business in order to protect the assets.

Types of Funding

- Personal Funding
- Commercial Bank Loans
- Small Business Administration Loan (SBA)
- Partnerships
- Investors
- Venture Capital
- Landlord Contributions
- Leasing
- Combination Financing

Personal Funding (100% Ownership)

In this scenario, all funds are provided by you personally. Believe it or not, this is the way a lot of first-timers open a restaurant, and as a result, their projects are generally smaller in nature. There are also ways to fully fund a restaurant with contributions from other entities, and we will cover this later under Combination Financing.

> *Advantages:* You have 100% ownership with no debt service. No loan applications are needed, and there is no waiting.

> *Disadvantages:* You are using personal funds.

Commercial Business Loans

First-time restaurateurs will find a commercial loan much harder to acquire because they have little to no history. If this is your second or third profitable restaurant, you will have a much easier time securing a commercial loan. Lending institutions want the security of past performances because bad debt is a black eye on their business. That said, every bank is different, and just because one says "No" does not mean the next won't say "Yes" to funding your project. Each lender looks at business models differently—it is a very subjective decision.

Typically, loans are based on a floating interest rate for a designated amount of years. Almost always, a percentage of the money invested, collateral and personal guarantees are required Partners will have the same requirements. Remember, this loan will need to be paid back whether your business succeeds or not.

Get applications from several local banking institutions and make appointments to meet with their lending officer. Search the Web—some lenders specialize in restaurant loans. Your first couple of interviews will give you a good indication of how you and your Business Plan are being perceived. Make sure you go to at least five lenders, and take great notes. You will begin to see some commonality to their understanding and perception of your model and will know if you need to make some adjustments to your presentation. Do not give up because of rejection. If you feel like each presentation is being better received than the last, go to a few more lenders. As I said before, first-timers have a hard time securing this type of loan.

Advantages: You can retain total ownership.

Disadvantages: Collateral and personal guarantees are required.

Small Business Administration Loan

SBA loans are an alternative to getting a traditional commercial loan. The 7(a) Loan Guarantee Program is designed for small businesses. The loans are given by the same lenders that execute commercial banking loans, so in order to qualify for an SBA, you would have had to apply for a commercial loan and been rejected. In other words, you may receive an SBA loan from the same bank that rejected you for a commercial loan. The reason for this is that these are government loans that are guaranteed to the lender in case of personal or business default, substantially reducing the risk to the lender. Loan amounts of $150,000 to $2,000,000 can be obtained. Loans for less than $150,000 are guaranteed at a higher guaranteed rate of interest. These loans are fully amortized, no down or minimum down payment is required, negotiable interest rates are regulated by SBA, there are no balloon payments, and there are no prepayment penalties if over three years. SBA loans can be long term. These loans are designed for 99% of the businesses in the United States, and only extremely large companies would be ineligible.

What Do You Need for an SBA Loan?

- ❐ Business model must prove that debt will be covered. Second-time owners will have an easier time with qualifying.
- ❐ You have applied for a commercial loan and were rejected.
- ❐ Business debt to net worth must meet industry averages and standards.
- ❐ Borrowers must be actively involved in the day to day operations of the funded business. Suitable personal credit history is required for all principals and guarantors.
- ❐ All owners with 20% ownership are required to personally guarantee the loan.
- ❐ No past bankruptcy or felony arrests.
- ❐ Your business is a for-profit entity.
- ❐ Some collateral, equity in business, and/or cash will be required to secure a loan.

Search the Web and educate yourself about the 7(a) SBA loan. Get applications from several local banking institutions and make appointments to meet with their lending officers. Make sure the banking institutions you apply to have the authority to approve an SBA 7(a) loan. Some lenders do not have the authority to approve an SBA loan. Your first couple of interviews will give you a good indication of how you and your Business Plan are perceived. Again, be sure to go to at least five lenders, and take great notes. Make some adjustments to your presentation as necessary, but don't give up because of rejection.

Advantages: These loans are designed for small businesses, you can apply to the same lender that handles commercial loans, long term loans are available for up to twenty-five years, and you can retain total ownership.

Disadvantages: Personal guarantees and collateral are required.

Partnerships

In law terms, a partnership is an association of two or more persons who have agreed to combine their labor, property, and skill (some or all of them) for the purpose of engaging in lawful business and sharing profits and losses between them. In this definition, the term "business" includes every trade, occupation, and profession.

This is the easiest way to raise money, and typically it is a natural fit. One partner might be the chef, one the manager, and another, the bartender. The nice thing about this arrangement is that each party brings expertise to the project. Partnerships can take on all types and forms, and this will be discussed later under Combination Financing. We will begin by concentrating on a typical partnership.

A typical partnership has at least two partners. Each partner contributes a share, not always equal, of the money it takes to open the restaurant. If you have a 50% equal partnership, each partner shares in costs, profits and losses equally. If the partnership is not equal, the share of costs, profits and losses will be distributed according to the percentage of ownership. For example, there might be an 80% owner and a 20% owner. The 80% share will have 80% of the costs, profits and losses. In most cases the majority partner has more authority, but that's not always true. Each partnership requires some agreed-upon legal definition of authority. There can be many partners, or just two. Many first-timers choose this as a way to start and then try other financing for a second location later when they have established a history that will enable them to get a commercial loan.

Your first choice for a partner may be someone who can not only contribute money but has some expertise that relates to your concept and vision. If you are opening a French restaurant, your first choice of partners might be a great chef. If you are already in the industry, you will have a great base for attracting partners with like ambition. Another good choice might be for partners that will not lend expertise but are willing to invest. They typically remain silent (which can be a benefit!). The money is out there, and if you can deal with the unique challenges of a partnership, this is a good way to start. Once you have an established history of running a profitable restaurant, you should be able to get financing on your own for your second restaurant.

Advantages: This is a way to fund your restaurant without the involvement of lending institutions. If you are the majority stock holder, you can generally make or veto all initiatives. There is generally added value in the way of professional expertise.

Disadvantages: "Too many cooks spoil the soup," partners sometimes don't get along, or one partner doesn't live up to their obligations. In most cases, the 20% owner will be just as responsible as the 80% owner when signing leases, personal guarantees and contracts. This is not fair perhaps, but true.

Investors

The essence of investing is to put money to use, by purchase or expenditure, in something that potentially offers a profitable return in the form of interest, income, or appreciation in value.

Most great chefs are backed with investor financing when they open a restaurant, and this is the preferred way for most restaurateurs to raise funds. The characteristics of this type of funding are a bit unique because what investors are most concerned about is their Return on Investment (ROI). It is purely based on risk vs. reward—they want to know that the up-side is much larger than what they could obtain from a bank fund. Unlike partnerships, you can raise money in a non-proportional way. For example, you can raise 100% of the funds needed to fund your restaurant through investors, and give 49% of the profits and ownership in return. Be aware that most investors want to make sure you also have money invested. They are banking on your expertise to return profits, and their expertise assures them they have a great chance to be profitable. Investors are reluctant to back a non-restaurant person or someone who has little experience in managing revenue.

A typical investor agreement includes a percentage of the profits and ownership. This is not a loan and will not get paid back. In other words, investors share in the loss as well as the profits. They will almost always refuse to sign any lease, vendor personal guarantees, or for that matter, any contracts other than the one they sign for an ownership percentage. Investors use a stock market mentality when investing, and are almost always silent partners. They understand that they are involved with profit and loss, but they don't want any liability.

Note: If your cash investment is borrowed money and you have a debt service, personal debt payment will be made with your share of the restaurant profits. Unless agreed upon, you will not be able to raise investor money by adding personal debt service to the cost of operating the restaurant.

The investors are looking for ROI. Following are a couple of examples.

Example 1

Imagine that you need to raise $500,000 to open your restaurant. Sales for the first year are projected at $1,500,000 with a profit of 15% ($225,000). That equals an ROI of 45%. If you decide you will sell up to 40% ownership and that each share will cost the investor $5,000 for a total of $200,000, the ROI for each share is 45% or $2,250. That is huge!

Example 2

Use the same sales and profit scenario as Example 1 with the exception of the cost of shares. You are still going to retain 60% ownership, but now the cost of shares is $7,500. $7,500 x 40 shares = $300,000. The ROI per share is still $2,250, but the ROI percentage has changed to 30%, which is still a big ROI. As a result you have raised 60% of the money from investors and returned 40% of the profits and ownership.

Remember, restaurants have a reputation for being risky. Investors in the foodservice industry will want to minimize their liability and maximize their ROI. An ROI of 30% is a good number to achieve. Treat investors well—for obvious reasons, they only want what is best for you. If you can return substantial profits, you will have investor money for the future as well. Always give your present investors the opportunity to get involved in future sites. In fact, most investors will write that into the contract. Examples 1 and 2 are just two of numerous scenarios that make up an investor agreement. Be fair and you will raise the money. Be greedy, and you know the result.

Advantages: You can retain a larger percentage of ownership, the investors are typically silent (you can also insist that they are silent), you have no debt service, and you have total control over operations. If treated well, investors are an endless resource, not only for money, but for valuable counsel.

Disadvantages: Investors will rarely sign leases or personal guarantees. The liability for business success is almost always yours alone because investors typically will not add expertise to your restaurant.

Venture Capital

Once you have several restaurants and have a great record of profitability, new financing options will be available to you. There are venture-capital firms that will take a hot concept and invest considerable funds for future sites. They typically want a greater share of partnership and will want to have considerable input on determining the direction of the concept and vision. They will want to see a large return within three to seven years.

Advantages: Expansion expertise, endless amount of funds, large CEO salary, future concepts, pot of gold at the end of the rainbow, invested money is not a loan.

Disadvantages: Loss of control, venture-capitalists can and will pull the plug at any time

The types of loans discussed above are very typical and available to the restaurant industry. You might want to search the Web for additional creative forms of lending but you will probably find them risky and hard to obtain. Following are ways of obtaining funds that are used in combination with the above lending practices. Most restaurateurs will use a combination of equity, contributions and loans for funding—the best way is to do whatever works for you. But before we discuss combination loans, I would like to touch on a few additional ways to raise money.

Landlords

Landlords are a good source of cash, and there are often many reasons why they will contribute funds. This will depend on many factors: the economy, your concept, personal history, expertise, permanent tenant improvements, and length of the lease. Almost always, landlords will offer some allowance in the form of money for improvements. These are typically designated for flooring, lighting and items that the lessee cannot take with them when they leave. The amount of money for improvements varies widely from nothing at all to as much as $10 or $40 per square foot. There is no rule of thumb when it comes to landlord improvements. Some landlords will give you a considerable amount of money in exchange for a guaranteed long-term lease. Some will give cash in exchange for an increase in rent. This really works well if your business model allows for additional rent payments. Maybe the landlord will fund the entire project in exchange for a guaranteed long-term lease and ownership. The point is that landlords are a good source of cash. If they have the resources to fund the building you are leasing, they will also have the resources to fund your restaurant. In order to get a landlord interested you need to win them over on many levels: a great concept and Business Plan, good financial history, expertise in your concept, and the impression that you are likeable and professional. Out of all the available lenders, your landlord is the one entity with whom you can negotiate. They will do everything in their power to get their space leased. In fact, the tougher the economy, the more you can get—the landlord wants you to succeed. Ask for an allowance for tenant improvements such as work on your ventilation system. Always get as much as the landlord is willing to give. Leave nothing on the table.

Advantages: Landlords are a great source of cash.

Disadvantages: You could end up with a long-term lease and/or higher rent.

Leasing

There are companies that specialize in leasing equipment and furnishing, but this is not a recommended way to fund a restaurant. The full package can be leased, but if your cost to open is $500,000, you may have an additional kitchen equipment package of $150,000. Generally leases are associated with high interest rates and a lessee with prior restaurant ownership. I would recommend not leasing more than one or two pieces of equipment. Dish machines are often leased because they are very expensive to buy and are considered high maintenance. You can lease a dish machine from your food supplier, a dish machine manufacturer, or a dish machine chemical company. The fees are inexpensive and sometimes include the purchase of detergents. The company that leases the dish machine is the same company that performs regularly scheduled maintenance. If the machine breaks down, they will fix it. That could help free up $7,000 to $50,000, depending on the size of machine. Another commonly leased item is an ice machine. They are also high maintenance and require regularly scheduled service calls. If the machine breaks down, some companies will supply you with ice until the machine is repaired. Beyond the dish and ice machines, I recommend funding your equipment by using other available resources. Rethink moving forward if you find yourself having to lease the majority of your equipment.

Advantages: Good for leasing high maintenance items such as a dish and ice machine.

Disadvantages: You may be required to buy the leasing company's detergents, pay very high interest rates on large equipment packages, have a history of restaurant ownership.

Combination Financing

The most common way restaurants are funded is by using a variety of methods for financing. For instance, on the one hand you can have either a partnership with investors, or sole ownership with landlord contributions and a leased dish machine, or on the other hand investors with landlord contributions and leases. The combinations are endless. Below is a typical scenario for using the investor business model.

- Funds required - $500,000.
- John and Jane Doe own 60% of the business.
- Investor Contribution - $300,000 at 40% ownership;
- Landlord Contribution - $5.00 per square foot totaling $20,000;
- Dish and Ice Machine Lease - $20,000;
- Funds needed from John and Jane Doe - $160,000.

You can see there are many ways to use combination funding. They are limitless! This is a great way to limit liability for any one party, but everyone has to be treated with equity and fairness.

Advantages: There are limitless resources, it is easier to attract limited funding and investors, it's a great way to fund a restaurant.

Disadvantages: Investors will not sign leases or give personal guarantees unless real estate ownership is involved, the liability is almost always yours alone, investors will not typically add any expertise to your restaurant.

Financing Summary

We have discussed many creative ways you can fund a restaurant. A combination of funding and sources may be the only way to fully finance, but if your concept and vision are solid and all aspects of your business model are enticing, you will get funded—no question about it. If you do your due diligence, you will generate an abundant amount of interest in your project. And remember, everything you do to obtain funding needs to be implemented with the highest level of integrity. I'd wish you good luck, but it's not "luck" that will get you funded. Successful funding lies in your abilities.

Until you are fully funded, do not sign leases, purchase equipment, employ designers or a general contractor, nor promise anyone money. Once funded, you've completed Phase 1 and will start executing Phase 2, your in-depth chronological map to realizing your dream. A good execution of Phase 2 will literally save you aggravation, time, and tens of thousands of dollars.

Note: I cannot give legal advice, but I suggest you contact an accountant to discuss and choose from the types of partnership agreements that are available (sole ownership, S-Corp., LLC, etc.) Contact a lawyer to create the appropriate contracts. Do not move forward without having these professionals in place.

Journal for Obtaining Financing

Lending Institution 1:_____
Lending Officer: _____
Address: _____
Phone(s): _____
E-mail: _____
Date of Interview: _____ Time of Interview:_____
Synopsis: _____
_____
_____
_____
_____

Lending Institution 2: _____
Lending Officer: _____
Address: _____
Phone(s): _____
E-mail: _____
Date of Interview: _____ Time of Interview:_____
Synopsis: _____
_____
_____
_____
_____

Lending Institution 3:_____
Lending Officer: _____
Address: _____
Phone(s): _____
E-mail: _____
Date of Interview: _____ Time of Interview:_____
Synopsis: _____
_____
_____
_____
_____

Lending Institution 4: _____
Lending Officer: _____
Address: _____
Phone(s): _____
E-mail: _____
Date of Interview: _____ Time of Interview:_____
Synopsis: _____
_____
_____
_____
_____

Lending Institution 5:_____

Lending Officer: _____

Address: _____

Phone(s): _____

E-mail: _____

Date of Interview: _____ Time of Interview:_____

Synopsis: _____

_____

_____

_____

Lending Institution 6:_____

Lending Officer: _____

Address: _____

Phone(s): _____

E-mail: _____

Date of Interview: _____ Time of Interview:_____

Synopsis: _____

_____

_____

_____

Investor 1: _____

Percentage Invested: _____

Address: _____

Phone(s): _____

E-mail: _____

Date of Interview: _____ Time of Interview:_____

Synopsis: _____

_____

_____

_____

Investor 2: _____

Percentage Invested: _____

Address: _____

Phone(s): _____

E-mail: _____

Date of Interview: _____ Time of Interview:_____

Synopsis: _____

_____

_____

_____

Investor 3: _____

Percentage Invested: _____

Address: _____

Phone(s): _____

E-mail: _____

Date of Interview: _____ Time of Interview:_____

Synopsis: _____

_____

_____

_____

Investor 4: _____

Percentage Invested: _____

Address: _____

Phone(s): _____

E-mail: _____

Date of Interview: _____ Time of Interview:_____

Synopsis: _____

_____

_____

_____

Investor 5: _____

Percentage Invested: _____

Address: _____

Phone(s): _____

E-mail: _____

Date of Interview: _____ Time of Interview:_____

Synopsis: _____

_____

_____

_____

Investor 6: _____

Percentage Invested: _____

Address: _____

Phone(s): _____

E-mail: _____

Date of Interview: _____ Time of Interview:_____

Synopsis: _____

_____

_____

_____

Funding Categories and Amounts

Category	Amount	Notes
Funds Needed		
Funders		
Landlord Contributions		
Leasing		
TOTAL FINANCING		

Notes

Notes

Instruction 4: *Site Selection*

Instruction 4: *Site Selection*

"LOCATION... LOCATION... LOCATION... "

— "WISE" ANONYMOUS

Where is the perfect site for your restaurant? There isn't one, of course, but with due diligence you can get pretty close. The right location is determined by all the possible factors that can affect costs and sales. For most restaurateurs, the perfect site is based on emotion, and I don't want to minimize that because it's a big part of your overall vision. Emotion and passion in the foodservice industry is a good thing. In the site selection process, you need to use a bit of emotion and a whole lot of logic. The bottom line to every successful business is the profit, and that's not always assured just because you have located your restaurant on the hottest corner in the city. The best location is not always the most practical. Purchasing land and constructing your restaurant or leasing a space is a long term risk. Many restaurant companies spend thousands of dollars on feasibility studies to determine great restaurant sites, but the smaller restaurateur can not afford that. Your local city hall and library will have demographic information like median incomes along with traffic counts and traffic pattern data. The information is out there for the taking. What really matters is that the site you have selected is going to give you the best chance for profitability. You have already completed a great Business Plan and you know, based on your model, what is affordable and gives you the best chance to succeed. The following information must be factored in before committing to a site.

Factors in Site Selection

- Location Statistics – municipality, demographics, median income, traffic patterns, foot traffic, blue collar business, white collar business, daytime population.

- Competition – restaurants, pricing, alcohol, concepts, service.

- Codes and Licensing – zoning requirements, titles, disability concerns, fire, waste, permitting, parking, flood plain, soil tests and landscaping greenery, liquor license availability, liquor license costs, liquor license laws, restrictions and food license.

- Location Attributes – retail anchors, shopping centers, sports facilities, hospitals, universities, schools, office complexes, restaurants, theaters, performing arts, parks and recreation destinations.

- Building and Lot – square footage, shape, end cap, visibility, building condition, utilities and mechanicals.

- Cost Comparables – appraisals, going-rate comparisons.

- Negotiations – site cost, cost per square foot, revenue per square foot, taxes, costs for common area maintenance (CAM), lease terms, tenant improvement allowance and landlord improvements.

As the topics suggest, the perfect site is made up of many considerations. I recommend that you detail each one so you will have assurance that you have selected the best site based on you concept and vision while adhering to your budget and giving yourself the best chance for profitability.

Location Statistics

- **Municipality**
  Is this the right town for your concept? New York, Chicago and LA are so diverse and large that virtually every concept will work. That is not true in other towns. There might be a very good reason that Bismarck, North Dakota does not have a raw bar. In order to have 100% certainty, you have to investigate.

  Can this market support your concept? Yes_____ No_____
  Describe your reasoning:

  _____
  _____
  _____
  _____
  _____
  _____
  _____
  _____

- **Demographics**

  Do the necessary investigative work to acquire population statistics. If the city you are proposing has a population of 30,000 people, ask the more specific question—is there a daytime population? This is essential for lunch time sales. Understand the foot traffic and vehicle traffic patterns. Just because you have a major highway going through town doesn't mean those people are stopping. You also need to know the median income of your population.

  Are there enough white collar businesses to support lunch sales? Yes_____ No_____

  Population:_____ Daytime Population:_____ Median Income:_____

  Traffic Patterns: Great ___ Good ___ Fair ___ Bad___

  Will the site demographics support your concept? Yes_____ No_____

  Describe your conclusion:

  _____

  _____

  _____

  _____

  _____

  _____

  _____

  _____

  _____

  _____

  Based on demographics, I have determined that this is a GREAT site for my new restaurant. Signature: _____

Note: If you feel the word GREAT does not accurately describe the selected location, keep looking for sites.

Competition

The best way to confirm your business model is by studying your local competition. Restaurants succeed for many different reasons and what makes you successful may be completely different than what makes your competition successful. By now you have determined that you have a sound concept, vision and business model for your new restaurant. You have studied the municipality and have selected the perfect setting. Your competition is your confirmation that this is where you belong, so spend time at the competing restaurants. Go there for breakfast, lunch and dinner to determine if the volume is adequate for your business model. Study the habits of the customers. Get a good feel for the sales and try to understand why one restaurant is wildly successful while their competition a couple of doors down is struggling. What you really want to determine is whether or not there are sales possibilities. Competition is good, and every average-sized city has one or more "restaurant rows" that bring business to the area. So don't be afraid to have an Italian restaurant in a city that already has like-concepts. In San Francisco you will find eight Italian restaurants in a row. In China Town there are fifty like-concepts within ten blocks. Each restaurant has its own little twists to the concept that makes it unique, and the price points or the level of service may not be the same. You don't necessarily have to be original, but you have to be good. Should you be the third Italian restaurant in a very small town like Victoria, Minnesota? All you might be doing is sharing customers who want Italian food that particular day. Create a great customer experience, and that will make you successful. Meanwhile, pull for and support your fellow restaurateurs—your competition can be your friend. There is plenty of business for everyone.

Consider the following before moving forward with a site selection:

Number of foodservice facilities in the area: _____

Number of like-concepts: _____

Number of restaurants with the same pricing: _____

Number of restaurants with like serving style: _____

Estimated sales of like-competition: _____

New competition planned or under construction: _____

Write a short essay to substantiate that your selected location can support your business model. Document and categorize your findings:

_____

_____

_____

_____

_____

_____

_____

_____

_____

Based on the competition, I have determined that this is a GREAT site for my new restaurant. Signature: _____

Note: If you feel the word GREAT does not accurately describe your selected location, keep looking for sites.

Codes and Licensing

- **Zoning**

  If you are purchasing land and constructing a building, you will need to know if it is zoned for the intended use. If you are leasing, the landlord will have that information. Is the site zoned for the intended use? Yes_____ No_____

- **Liquor License**

  Every town and city has different liquor license standards, laws and pricing. If a license is required, is one available and can you qualify for it? Some cities require you to sell food with liquor, some have a separate beer and wine license, and some require that the restaurant be at least 300 feet away from a school and/or church. All have different costs. In New Jersey you may have to purchase a liquor license from an individual. Those licenses are owned and can cost as much as $300,000. In most areas you secure the license from the city in which you are operating, and those can be as little as $2,000/year. You need to get the facts so you don't break the budget. Remember, the city you select should be an asset, not an obstacle. Decide if the liquor license requirements and cost will prohibit you from achieving profits as suggested by your business model. Example: Cost of liquor for the year is $40,000, liquor labor costs $40,000, annual liquor license $10,000, liquor liability insurance $12,000. Total liquor costs without rent considerations = $102,000. Liquor sales for the year is $200,000. You can clearly see profitability in this example.

  Is a liquor license available? Yes _____ No _____

  Annual liquor license fee: $ _____

  Are there any restrictions on your liquor license? Yes _____ No _____

  If "Yes," list the restrictions: _____

  _____

  _____

  _____

  Do the liquor profits match your business model? Yes _____ No _____

- **Code Requirements**

  If you are purchasing land and constructing a building, you will need to hire an architect immediately. The architect, along with other professionals, has the resources and expertise to address the following code concerns: Clear Titles, ADA Accessibility Requirements, Fire Codes, Soil Tests, Parking Lot Size, Water, Sewage, Utility Availability, Flood Plain, HVAC, Landscaping, Greenery, Ingress and Egress, Geological Survey, Building Height, Setback Restrictions, Sight Codes, Signage Codes, Leveling, Grading and Fill Requirements. It is beyond the typical restaurateur's expertise to assemble the required code information. The experts needed to address these issues must be part of your land and building budget. Do not purchase land unless all your code, utility and zoning information has been addressed.

If you are leasing, most of the code requirements have already been addressed by the landlord. It will be up to you to investigate utility availability, customer egress, HVAC, parking and possibly other code considerations. Do not sign a lease unless you have the necessary information to move forward without having to make alterations to your business model.

All of this might seem a bit mind-boggling, but it doesn't have to be. Get the right people involved and it is easy. Just make sure you have addressed all the issues (using experts where needed) before moving forward.

Based on codes and licensing, I have determined that this is a GREAT site for my new restaurant. Signature: _____

Note: If you feel the word GREAT does not accurately describe your selected location, keep looking for sites.

Location Attributes

What will other industries contribute to the success of your restaurant? If your proposed restaurant site is in a sleepy community, your potential customers may be limited to local residents and drive-by traffic. Or perhaps your restaurant is so exceptional that people will come to you ("build it and they will come"). Is that enough volume for your business model? Most restaurants need to have other businesses and events in the area that generate a great deal of traffic. If your restaurant has 250 seats, you need to have supporting infrastructure to assure success. Spooner, Wisconsin can support a 60-seat café but probably will not be able to support a jazz nightclub that seats 250. You won't find a professional baseball team in Fargo, North Dakota because the population cannot support the business model.

Here is a listing of infrastructure that invites business to a given location: universities, schools, hospitals, professional and amateur sports teams, convention centers, theaters, performing arts centers, live music, office complexes, blue collar industry, major retail anchors, parks and recreation sites, museums, other restaurants, intense population, major thoroughfare, and other contributing activities.

List the infrastructure that could draw potential customers to your restaurant:

1. _____
2. _____
3. _____

4. _____

5. _____

6. _____

7. _____

8. _____

9. _____

10. _____

11. _____

Continually justify your decision-making-process with good documentation. Write a short essay to substantiate that the selected location can support your business model.

_____

_____

_____

_____

_____

_____

_____

_____

_____

_____

_____

_____

_____

_____

_____

_____

_____

_____

_____

_____

_____

Based on local attributes, I have determined that this is a GREAT site for my new restaurant. Signature: _____

Note: If you feel the word GREAT does not accurately describe the selected location, keep looking for sites.

Building and Lot

You have already determined the perfect building for your restaurant through the Concept and Vision and the Business Plan Instructions. You have confirmed that the demographics meet your business model, and that there are no code issues or zoning restrictions that could hinder your plans or result in higher than estimated costs. All the necessary licenses are available and meet your projected costs. The competition does well and will actually be an asset to your sales. There is more than enough business, theater, retail and recreational activity in the area to attract customers that will frequent your site.

You have now finished the intellectual portion of your site selection and are ready to choose a building. There are many questions to consider in selecting the right building for your concept. For example, does the square footage and shape of the space match your concept, vision and business model? There are also questions regarding code concerns, ADA considerations, utility requirements, grease trap requirements, sewer and water accessibility costs, accessible ventilation locations, and legal egress issues. Do you need an end cap for a drive-thru or a patio area? If you are purchasing a lot and constructing a building, you have already covered some of the following topics with your architect. Each concern has to be addressed before considering a site. As shown earlier, the most attractive building is not always the best. And there are always long term implications. You don't want to purchase an existing building or sign a lease and find out later that your one-time sewer and water hookup fee is $45,000—a fee that most first time restaurateurs don't even know exists. If this and the next two topics are executed with the utmost diligence, you will save tens of thousands of dollars. If not, the results can be absolutely catastrophic.

Most of the following topics are questions that have associated costs. They are not given in any particular order. Do not move forward until all of the questions have been adequately answered.

- **Condition of the Building**
  Is the building in good repair? Are there any leaks in the roof or other structural issues? Are there any code issues? Hire an inspector at the landlord's or owner's expense to inspect the site, and then make sure they agree in writing to make repairs and bring the building up to code. Sometimes tenants are held responsible for roofs and exteriors of a building once the lease is signed, and you don't want that responsibility. Make sure the exterior facade of the building is in "opening" condition, and that all the windows and doors are presentable and in good repair. Make sure the heating and air-conditioning units are in good working order and will last for the term of your lease. Always have your landlord warranty the units in writing—leasing agents are good at telling half truths, and this is a budget-killer if not considered . This is one area where you may get a financial allowance from the landlord for bringing the building up to good repair. If this is the case, get all the necessary quotes in writing before accepting a funding agreement from

the landlord. Don't be afraid to ask for a building that's in perfect condition. It is not your building and you are not liable for repairs. You may be in for a big fight, but don't be bullied. Remember, there are other sites out there.

Note: All foodservice facilities will require some in-ground plumbing lines. In new construction sites the contractors will leave the floor open until all the mechanical lines are installed. If the floor is intact, you will need to have concrete cutting performed to accommodate plumbing lines and possibly soda lines, beer lines and electrical.

Is the building in good repair? Yes_____ No_____
Is it in compliance with building, structural, electrical, plumbing or ADA codes?
Yes_____ No_____
If "No," will the landlord remedy all repairs and code violations at their own expense?
Yes_____ No_____
If "No," you will want to seriously consider passing on the property.
Notes:

_____
_____
_____
_____
_____
_____
_____
_____
_____
_____
_____
_____
_____
_____
_____
_____
_____
_____
_____
_____
_____

- **Esthetics**

  Beauty is in the eye of the beholder. The important thing is that the building is conducive to your concept and vision. Some concepts call for large windows for great visibility, but that might be less important for other concepts. Tap the expertise of your design team to help make those types of decisions. As already stated, the building should be in good repair regardless of what your concept is.

  Notes:

  _____

  _____

  _____

  _____

- **Gas/LP and Electric**

  Your restaurant concept may have certain electrical and gas/LP requirements. Your concept drawing will help you get estimates from mechanical contractors on the electrical and gas/LP loads. Every foodservice venue has different requirements. Generally speaking a landlord will supply a retail space with the minimum amount of utilities. For instance, a 3,000 square foot space will be supplied with a 100 amp service. A 3,000 square foot restaurant will require a 200 or 300 amp service. Most landlords are not willing to pay for more than the minimum. Negotiate hard for this addition. This cost should be associated with construction in your Business Plan.

  1. **Gas/LP**

     What type of fuel is there to produce flames? Natural Gas_____ LP_____

     Other: _____

     How many BTUs are required for your concept?_____

     What size gas line is needed? _____

     Are the required BTUs already at the site? Yes _____ No _____

     If "No," what is the cost? $_____

     Does the gas line size need to be increased? Yes _____ No _____

     If "Yes," what is the cost? $_____

  2. **Electric**

     Does your concept require three-phase electrical? Yes _____ No _____

     Is three-phase at your site? Yes _____ No _____

     If "No," what is the cost to bring it in? $_____

     What voltage is available to the building? 120V___ 208V single-phase___

     208V three-phase___ 480V three-phase___ Other: _____

     Other: _____ Other: _____

How much amp service is needed, including HVAC, for your concept?_____

Is the required amp service already at the site? Yes ____ No _____

If "No," what is the cost? $_____

Notes: _____

_____

_____

_____

_____

_____

_____

_____

_____

_____

_____

- **Water and Sewer**

Every state, county and city has different rules and costs associated with the use and disposal of water. This can get a little complicated and be a real budget buster. Sometimes even the most veteran restaurateurs don't know beforehand that some of these charges exist. Sewer and water connection charges definitely need to be a part of your construction costs, but here is the kicker—there are different rules that apply so not everyone has to pay for this charge. If you are purchasing an existing restaurant, there likely are no charges—the connection fee has already been paid by the original operator. If you are purchasing or leasing a building that was previously used for retail, you will have to pay the connection fee. Similarly, if you are constructing or leasing a new building, you will have to pay the connection fee. In the case of gas and electrical, the landlord will always bring in the minimum required amount for the building based on a retail space. This means that only a small portion of the sewer and water connection charges have been paid by the landlord. For example, if your restaurant is in Blaine, Minnesota, you pay SAC and WAC Charges (a Sewer Availability Charge and Water Availability Charge). For a 150-seat full service restaurant, the fee is $38,977. That is a big number that is rarely budgeted for. If your restaurant site is in Cocoa Beach, Florida, the fee will be in excess of $22,200. Almost every area has charges for Sewer and Water connections. Many municipalities want the funds paid up front, but some will let you spread the fee out over time. If you are on a self-owned well and septic system, still different rules apply and there might not be any charges.

Grease traps also need to be considered. Each municipality has different rules and costs. Some cities do not require them, some require outdoor grease traps, and some require indoor grease traps.

Water and sewer lines need to be appropriate for your consumption rate. There may be a cost associated with this.

The bottom line is that there are considerable costs associated with water consumption and waste disposal. As stated, each municipality is different so make sure you have all the necessary costs before moving forward. This is a component of your pre-opening construction costs. You may be able to negotiate these fees with your landlord—it's often a hard sell but definitely worth exploring.

Sewer connection:	Fee $_____	Does not apply ____
Water connection:	Fee $_____	Does not apply ____
Sewer line:	Fee $_____	Does not apply ____
Water line:	Fee $_____	Does not apply ____
Outdoor grease trap: Size _____	Fee $_____	Does not apply ____
Indoor grease trap: Size _____	Fee $_____	Does not apply ____

Notes (Water and Sewer):

_____

_____

_____

_____

_____

_____

_____

_____

- **HVAC** (Heating, ventilation and air-conditioning)
  Does your selected building provide easy access to ventilation? Hood ventilation is strictly regulated by the city, health and fire departments. Before we discuss the building requirements, you need to be educated on exhaust hoods and how they work. In the food-service industry, there are three very common types of ventilation and each has different uses. In some high-rise applications, they may also require ultraviolet technology. Check with the leasing company about UV requirements.

  1. **Direct Vent** is only allowed in an application that releases dry heat. The only time we see these allowed is in a bakery operation where they are strictly baking breads.

  2. **Type 1 Vent** is required for all cooking equipment that produces grease-laden

vapors. There are no exceptions. This also applies to electric cooking equipment. Type 1 hoods require welded black iron ducting that is surrounded with an approved blanket-type wrapping or an approved fire-resistant drywall wrap. Equipment such as fryers, ranges, steamers, ovens, broilers and griddles will require a Type 1 hood. Type 1 hoods will almost always require a fire suppression system.

3. **Type 2 Vent** is for ventilating condensation. Dishwashers are typically required to have a Type 2 hood. In a certain town in New Jersey (which will remain nameless), they even require a Type 2 hood over a coffee urn. With some exceptions you may be allowed to vent a "stand alone" steam kettle with a Type 2 hood. Type 2 hoods do not require the welded black iron duct, fire wrapping, or a fire suppression system.

Every city will require you to have "make-up air" if you are doing any venting. By definition, make-up air is the replacement of exhausted air. In other words, the amount of air exhausted through your hoods and even the bathroom exhaust fans needs to be replaced with fresh make-up air. Some cities require that the make-up air is cooled or heated, depending on you geographical location. If you are exhausting 5,000 cfms (cubic feet per minute) of air, the city will require you to replace 80% of it. If you are opening a coffee shop and are not cooking or using a dishwasher, you will not need ventilation hoods or make-up air.

There is also equipment designed to reduce odor. If required, the odor abatement system takes the exhaust and runs it through a device that substantially reduces odors. They are required in some big cities and the surrounding suburbs. Check with local environmental codes. This is not a cheap piece of equipment.

Now that you understand the types of hoods involved in a restaurant, you need to understand how the ductwork is vented through the building. There are really only two ways to vent: up through the roof or through a side wall. Keep in mind that the longer the duct, the more expensive it will be. This is especially true for Type 1 hoods. Ducting up to the roof is found in about 90% of today's restaurants, while ducting through a side wall is allowed on very few occasions. What type of building is most conducive to venting? The answer is, a single story building. Are you leasing a space with floors above you? If "Yes," you have to make sure there is a way to vent to the roof. Some landlords provide a mechanical shaft to the roof, and some don't. If you have five floors above you and the landlord has provided a way to vent to the roof, you are good to go. If not, I would suggest you pass on that site. Also, remember that the cost is going to be much higher if there are floors above your restaurant. Have you allowed for that additional cost in your budget? You have to decide if those floors above you will be cost effective. Maybe there is a major business or residential units that will create income, or maybe not. In regards to ventilation issues, weigh all of your conditions and options. Poor decision could result in thousands of dollars being wasted.

Are you venting through a roof? Yes _____ No _____ Through a sidewall? Yes _____ No _____

If roof, how many floors are above the restaurant? _____

If there are floors above the restaurant, is there a way to get to the roof through the floors above? Yes _____ No _____

Is make-up air required? Yes _____ No _____ Cooled? _____ Heated? _____

Is an odor abatement system required? Yes _____ No _____

Are there any special hoods such as UV required? Yes _____ No _____

Notes:

_____
_____
_____
_____
_____
_____
_____
_____
_____

- **Legal Egress**

  This is a term used for exiting. Today's general code requires that restaurants with 15 seats or more are required to have two means of egress for emergency use. Some very large restaurants may require three means of egress. Everything depends on the code requirements for the city you're in. Different formulas are used to determine the maximum distance required to exit. The codes also state that customers cannot walk through a kitchen to get to the exit. The exit has to be free and clear of all working areas, so if you are in a strip mall and the space is narrow and long, you will have some design issues. Perhaps a hallway needs to be created for customer exiting. Being a common issue, this is rarely a challenge for a good foodservice designer. If you have an end cap, you can have exiting through the side that leads to a patio, which is a good use for a legal egress. Spaces with only one entrance/exit will almost always be used for light retail, thus eliminating foodservice venues.

  Are there two free and clear means of egress? Yes _____ No _____

  If "Yes," does it conflict with your use of space, concept and vision? Yes _____ No _____

  Notes:

  _____
  _____
  _____
  _____

- **Handicap Accessibility**

  Almost all towns adhere to the standards that have been set by the Americans with Disabilities Act (ADA). The only exceptions to the ADA standards are buildings that are historic in nature or were "grandfathered in." If you are converting an old fire house into a restaurant, you will probably be required to follow all the ADA standards. If you are buying an existing restaurant and doing minor changes, they may relax the ADA standards. Most buildings built in the last 30 years will already have handicap accessibility. Check with a local agency for specific ADA requirements pertaining to your selected building. Many restaurants occupy more than one floor, and if that is the case, you must supply equal access according to ADA standards. It may require the installation of an elevator. If your design requires a floor elevation, you may be required to have a ramp for handicap accessibility. Your design team will help you verify all the ADA code requirements. Just make sure that you understand the city requirements for handicap accessibility because every city interprets the code differently. Most landlords will bring their building up to code, but handicap accessibility issues that are created by design features are always at the expense of the restaurateur.

  Your design team will address all of the ADA codes when designing your restaurant. Aisle ways, egress, elevations and restrooms will all be discussed throughout the design process. Concerning restrooms, they must be handicap accessible. In fact, one of the requirements is to have a space with a five-foot clear radius large enough for a wheel chair to turn. Restaurants with less than 15 seats may require only one unisex restroom. Generally, operations with over 15 seats will require both men's and women's ADA-compliant restrooms. The more seating there is, the larger the restrooms have to be. If you are a large restaurant, you may also be required to have an employee-ADA compliant bathroom.

  Have I investigated and understood all the city handicap accessibility requirements?
      Yes_____ No_____

  Does the building selected for the restaurant meet all the handicap accessibility code
      requirements? Yes _____ No _____

  If "No," can the building be brought up to code at the landlord's expense?
      Yes _____ No _____

  Notes:

  _____

  _____

  _____

  _____

  _____

Cost Comparables

Before you enter into negotiations with the leasing agent or a landlord, you have to know what you are willing to pay for rent. With the help of a real-estate agent, go to several available spaces and get leasing information and costs even though it is difficult to know what a landlord will give you until you enter into the hard negotiating stage. The general information you want is cost per square foot and the Common Area Maintenance (CAM) charges per square foot. CAM charges include taxes, plowing, landscaping and maintenance to the exterior of the building. Once you have received several quotes, you will get an idea of the going rates. Select at least three sites that are favorable to your concept and vision. Determine not to get emotionally involved in any particular site by considering all of them as equal in status. You need to have answered all of the above information (building condition, gas/LP and electric, water and sewer, HVAC, egress, ADA and aesthetics) before you begin negotiations. The big question is, "Does this site reflect my concept and vision, meet all the necessary code requirements, and fit well within my budget and business model?" If the answer is "Yes," proceed to the negotiation stage as outlined below. If "No," you must go back and address the issues. Do not exceed your budget or compromise your business model—investors will not take well to making any concessions when it comes to their ROI (Return on Investment). We have talked about how making decisions based on emotion is sometimes a good thing, but decisions regarding site location can only be based on logic and reason.

Negotiations

When you have gathered all the necessary information and are sure of your site choice, you are ready to move forward with negotiations. This section is going to focus primarily on leasing space. You have a good understanding of the demographic statistics—you have studied your competition and are convinced that your concept and vision will have similar results You've also found that there is a liquor license available and the cost is well within your business model and budget, plus there is plenty of local business and activity in the area to assure brisk sales. You have selected at least three sites that have all the necessary utilities and attributes and will keep you within your construction budget. You know what the going rate is for leasing space in the selected area, and you realize this is a long-term commitment.

Before going into hard negotiations, you have to know the highest amount you will pay for rent and CAM (Common Area Maintenance). That is the key. You must also have a list of items you want included in the lease. Dress appropriately and speak with clarity. Landlords and leasing agents are experienced negotiators and will not be surprised at your requests. Be firm in your demands or they will take the upper hand. Just be sure you are equipped to justify your demands. You are not asking for anything other tenants have not received.

Following is a list of possible scenarios you might want to consider when negotiating a lease.

- **Lease Costs**

  The lease cost is determined by square footage of the space leased. If the space is 3,000 square feet and the cost is $20 per square foot, your total annual cost will be $60,000. Most leases are increased yearly so make sure it is a fixed increase. Some landlords will insist on 5% of your income over the base lease.

  Example: The space is 3,000 square feet and the cost is $20 per square foot for a total annual cost of $60,000. Your sales for the year are $1,500,000, and 5% of $1.5 million is $75,000. You are now required to pay an additional $15,000 in rent. If your sales are only $1,000,000, your landlord will still collect the $60,000 even though 5% of the sales total is $50,000. This is a very common practice that you may or may not agree with. I, for one, have a real problem with this practice. Essentially your landlord becomes you partner and is allowed to audit your financial statements. You lose your privacy. You may not have a choice depending on where you're located—the bigger the city, the more likely you are to pay percentage-rent. The good thing is that your rent is generally well within your business model. I do believe you can ask the landlord for more allowances if you are indeed subjected to percentage-rent terms. The important thing here is that your rent costs fall well within your business model.

- **CAM** (Common Area Maintenance)

  Generally this includes property tax, exterior building maintenance, exterior lighting, landscaping, and parking lot care. In some areas, CAM may include waste removal, but it rarely includes HVAC maintenance. The fees vary greatly. A typical fee may be $5+ per square foot. Based on 3,000 square feet, the yearly CAM fee would then be $15,000.

- **Lease Terms**

  Read the fine print. For example, you will be using the roof for exhaust ventilation and most landlords will want roofs and all HVAC equipment listed as part of your responsibility. Repaving and re-striping the parking lot might be included in the CAM charges or might be an assessed charge. Is upgrading the building with a new facade included in the CAM charges, or is it an assessed charge? It's also common for a landlord to charge for managing the CAM fee and for billing you at the end of the year for overages. Again, make sure you understand the fine print.

- **Lease Length**

  There are many schools of thought on the ideal length for a lease. You can take any approach you want, but the result has to be favorable for the long haul. The longer the lease commitment, the more allowances you should be given for financial improvements. The only way to protect your investment is with long term lease guarantees. Most of the cost associated with opening a restaurant is due to the cost of the infrastructure, and the only thing you can reasonably take with you if you decide to leave is the equipment and furnishings. If the landlord is going to contribute considerable dollars, they will want a minimum five-year lease. That may be perfectly acceptable but the question is, "What happens after the five-year lease is up? Do you have options to renew?" You'd better have! If you don't have any options, your landlord can ask you to leave or he can raise your rent through the roof. Remember you can't take very much with you if you leave. In my opinion, the shorter the lease the better. You could have, for example, a three-year lease with ten three-year options, or even a five-year lease with five five-year options. There are many conceivable scenarios that will result in a secure lease. The bottom line is that you want the maximum amount of protection with the least amount of liability.

- **Personal Guarantees and Right to Sell**
  Every landlord will insist that you personally guarantee the terms of the lease. You must resist! However, the truth is that you probably won't be able to. What you can do, though, is insist that you will personally guarantee only the first term of the lease and not the option years. You can also insist on a buyout of the lease. A typical buyout is six months or a year. If you have a buyout clause, you can leave with a check in hand for the terms of the buyout. Once you have entered into a lease you should feel like you are a business owner and your restaurant is a saleable asset. If your lease is worded wrong, your restaurant is only a limited saleable asset. You must, and I mean must, have the right to sell your restaurant, and the buyer must have the right to assume your lease terms. This is easier said than done, however, and most landlords will not allow this. They are afraid you will sell to an unqualified, uneducated buyer for practically nothing just to get out of the lease. I don't blame them—I would have the same fear. What you can put into writing is that you are allowed to sell your restaurant at any time to a financially qualified buyer, and that you will guarantee the lease for a period of two years. After the two years is up, the lease and its terms will be transferred to the new tenant. I would not sign a lease without this clause or something similar. Otherwise the landlord will hold you hostage, insisting that you guarantee the full length of the lease as well as the option years. They will almost always extort money from you. "Extort" is a strong word, but that is exactly what your landlord will do. If they want your great restaurant in their space, they must concede to limiting personal guarantees and allow for a reasonable sale of your restaurant. Your Business Plan will have an exit strategy, and this is a major part of it. Always have a lawyer review the lease. Limit your liability. If you own your own building, this is obviously not an issue.

- **Warranties**
  In new construction sites, the equipment manufacturers will warranty the equipment for at least a year, and generally, longer. That is not a landlord warranty. If you are leasing a space in which the air-conditioning units are six years old, who is to say they're in good working order? Your landlord will allow you to have the AC unit inspected for good repair, but the truth is that the AC unit can completely fall apart the day after you

open and then it becomes your responsibility to replace it. Is that fair? Not in my estimation. Without warranties in place, you could have some serious budget-buster problems. Instead, have the landlord warranty all the mechanical equipment for at least a year, and that includes all existing heating and AC units. They aren't going to want to warranty the units, so your response is (said in a friendly tone), "Okay, replace the units. I would like the same new units the first tenant received." And remember to get all warranties in writing.

- **Leasehold Improvements**
Landlords will normally contribute funds for tenant improvements. The allowance is typically required to be used for infrastructure or for items that cannot be removed from the premises. You are apt to get more if the site is new and under construction. If it is an older site, the landlord will claim that the tenant improvement allowance was previously used by past tenants. Landlords or leasing agents will avoid this subject, so be prepared to fight for improvement funds. In a typical space, a landlord may allow three tons of air-conditioning for every 1,000 square feet of space. That is not enough for a restaurant application. And why would you want to pay for something that you will never be able to take with you? These are the types of improvements you will want to negotiate. In new construction, a landlord will give you considerable amounts of money to finish the space to your specifications. They will provide an HVAC, ceiling, lighting, flooring and give you a restroom allowance. This is a predetermined allowance based on a typical retail space, and if you accept those funds, it will then become your responsibility to upgrade the space for a restaurant application. Be sure to verify the allowance they give you with actual quotes on the items designated for funding. There is no set amount a landlord will offer—it could be $2 or $100 per square foot. Fight for as much as you can get, and remember, you can't take it with you. If the building is older, it is understandable why you will get less.

- **Date of Commencement (free rent)**
In a tough economy, you can get considerable free rent. To find out if this is a possibility in your case, investigate many properties. How much free rent are landlords willing to give? The better your data and your negotiating skills, the more you will receive. Do not accept anything less than free rent until the day your restaurant opens. This is a very common practice! Most landlords will insist on a precise number of days, so don't underestimate how long it will take to open.

There are many different ways to assure good pricing and landlord contributions. As already stated, your main goal is to not exceed your construction budget or jeopardize the integrity of your business model. Negotiate with a clear and educated vision.

Examples of Lease Agreements

Scenario 1

You have agreed to a five-year lease at $20 per square foot. Based on your business model, you know that the first year will yield fewer profits. Your proposal may be $16 for year one, and $21 for years two, three, four and five. Remember that years two, three, four and five may have an additional cost of living increase in the rent.

Scenario 2

You have agreed to a five-year lease at $20 per square foot based on a 3,000 square foot area. Your total rent, not including cost of living increases, is $300,000. You might request $50,000 in additional landlord funds to be used for infrastructure costs. In return, your suggested payback to the landlord could be rent increases in years two, three, four and five that would equal the extra $50,000 of infrastructure costs. Be sure, though, that the extra rent payments are within your operating budget.

Scenario 3

You are short on funds and require an investor. You might ask the landlord to complete the entire infrastructure package (plumbing, HVAC, electrical, flooring and finishes) in exchange for a slight increase in rent and a percentage of ownership. Landlords are partners in many restaurants—this is not an unusual practice. It is up to you to impress the landlord with your concept, vision and business model. You are more likely to achieve this in a building owned by an individual or a small group.

As you can imagine, there are innumerable scenarios that can result in a signed lease. Negotiate with your landlord in good faith. You will want to go into a negotiation session more educated than either the leasing agent or the landlord. Always be sure your data is undisputed, and leave no stone unturned. If you do your due diligence, you will be rewarded with a great lease and a great relationship with your landlord.

Notes

Instruction 5: *Key Personnel*

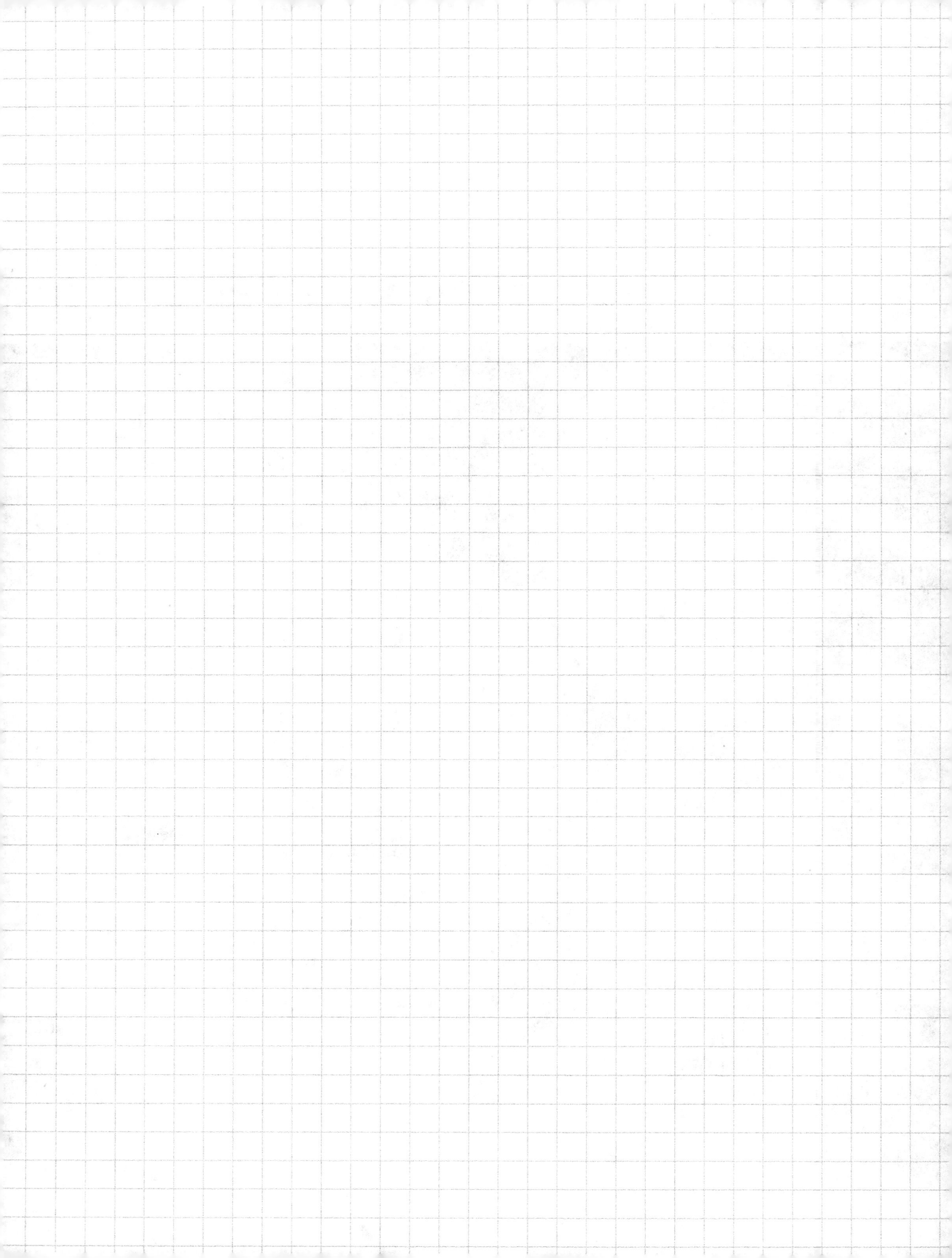

Instruction 5: *Key Personnel*

"Start with good people, lay out the rules, communicate with your employees, motivate them and reward them. If you do all those things effectively, you can't miss."

— Lee Iacocca

Congratulations! You have completed all of the Phase One Instructions and have signed your name on a lease. You are now on the fast track! All of the subsequent Instructions will in some ways need to be completed simultaneously. For example, hiring key employees may seem a bit premature, and in some cases it is, but in most cases the complexity of your restaurant will require one or more early hires. For that reason, please read this entire chapter before moving on to the next Instruction. There are many pre-opening tasks that you may not have the expertise to complete on your own. For instance, a great restaurant designer can design your kitchen without any input from the chef, but I guarantee that the chef will require some changes. Therefore, you might be better off hiring a chef sooner rather than later. If you have partners, one may be the chef and the other the bar manager. If that is the case, you don't need to hire any key employees early.

Key personnel procurement is going to depend on the complexity, size and concept of your operation. If your space is a small diner and you are the owner/chef, you may decide to hold off on early hiring. On the other hand, a fine dining restaurant with a large catering and banquet facility will require you to hire three or four key employees months before opening. Those key employees will help facilitate all the different pre-opening responsibilities. This doesn't necessarily mean they have to be hired full time initially. Some will lend their expertise as a consultant on a part time basis until just prior to opening. There are many different scenarios. A chef could be hired early to help design the menu, work with the kitchen designers, organize procedure manuals, interview kitchen personal, and research foodservice purveyors. That is a lot of responsibility for an owner in a larger facility, especially if he/she does not have the expertise of a chef. Your concept and size of space will definitely dictate the need for early hires. What if you tried to hire a great chef just four weeks prior to opening? The result could be chaos! The better plan is to hire key personnel early if possible. When you start the interview process early, you will assure yourself the best possible candidate. If your concept is fine dining, your chef will be a big part of the success. Don't try to do everything yourself—rely on the people who are going to make you successful. Of course, the early hires must be factored into your pre-opening budget.

The following list illustrates some of the typical foodservice concepts with their respective key personel. The number of key employees you will need to hire early in the process depends not only on the size of the space but also on your own areas of expertise.

- Coffee Shop: Manager/Owner and Barista.

- Deli: Manager/Owner and Deli Chef.

- Pizzeria: Manager/Owner and Pizza Chef.

- Ice Cream Parlor: Manager/Owner.

- Café: Manager/Owner and Café Chef.

- Diner: Manager/Owner and Chef.

- Casual Restaurant: Manager/Owner, Chef, and Dining Room Manager.

- Small Upscale Restaurant: Manager/Owner, Chef, Dining Room Manager, and Bar Manager.

- Large Upscale Restaurant: Owner, Food and Beverage Director, Executive Chef, Sous Chef, Office Manager/Controller, Dining Room Manager, Wine Steward, and Bar Manager.

- Large Upscale Restaurant with Banquet Facility: Owner, Food and Beverage Director, Executive Chef, Sous Chef, Office Manager/Controller, Dining Room Manager, Wine Steward, Bar Manager, Banquet Manager, and Marketer.

- Institutional Foodservice Facility: Manager, Chef, Dining Room Manager, and Nutritionist.

Every foodservice facility has similarities, but they are also different in many ways. They can be owned by highly skilled individuals, or their owners might not have any foodservice management experience. Only you can judge whether or not early hires will be required. Job descriptions for the above can vary greatly. If your concept is a brew pub, you will need a great brewer to produce your product. Maybe you have a big entertainment value in your concept that will require an expert in booking music acts. If you are a banquet facility, you will want a banquet manager and/or staff to book banquets months before you open. Don't wait until the eleventh hour—you will need to act quickly in order to procure the best possible prospects. The more complex and larger the space, the more expertise will be needed. Again, this is a component of your pre-opening budget.

Key Personnel to Consider for Early Hiring

- **Food and Beverage Director**
  Manager of all food and beverage operations; generally associated with large foodservice facilities, hotels and resorts.

- **Executive Chef**
  Manager of all food production and foodservice employees.

- **Dining Room Manager**
  Manager in charge of dining room procedures and waitstaff.

- **Head Chef/Chef**
  Person in charge of food production and kitchen staff. The word "chef" has been diluted over the years. For example, a cook working the grill at a fast-food establishment is some-times called a chef. By definition, "chef" is short for the French term, *chef de cuisine,* and means "head of the kitchen."

- **Sous Chef**
  Assistant chef, second in charge of food production and staff. Usually associated with medium- to high-volume restaurants.

- **Controller**
  Chief accounting officer. Generally associated with large facilities.

- **Bar Manager**
  Manager in charge of liquor sales, ordinary production, staff.

- **Banquet Manager**
  Manager in charge of banquet bookings and staff. Sometimes in charge of banquet marketing.

- **Wine Steward**
  A highly qualified expert in wine. In charge of the wine menu, marketing and inventory. They may have a staff in some cases.

- **Brewer**
  Expert in beer brewing production.

- **Office Manager**

  Manager in charge of general bookkeeping, HR responsibilities, employee policy, and procedure manuals. Could be employed by any medium- to high-volume facility.

- **Marketing**

  Person in charge of marketing all aspects of the foodservice facility. Typically associated with large multi-use facilities.

- **Barista**

  In the case of a possible early-hire, this should be someone with expertise in coffee and brewing.

- **Nutritionist**

  Generally required in health care, schools, and assisted living facilities.

- **Others**

  Any key employee that is necessary and vital to your concept and vision. This employee could be someone with expertise in booking live music acts, running a bowling alley, or other key ingredients to your concept. Only you can be the judge of this.

  Use the following checklist to plan your hiring. Remember, not all pre-hires need to start at the same time.

Checklist of Employees for Early Hiring

Position	Yes	N/A	Date
Food and Beverage Director			
Executive Chef			
Dining Room Manager			
Head Chef/Chef			
Sous Chef			
Controller			
Bar Manager			
Banquet Manager			
Wine Steward			
Brewer			
Office Manager			
Other:			

Notes

Instruction 6: *Design Team*

Instruction 6: *Design Team*

> "The design process is the management of constraints...
> The design process is conflict resolution."

> — DINO DINI, DESIGNER

What is design? After searching high and low for a great definition of "design," I have concluded that it is philosophical in nature. Like the word "love," it is hard to simply define. Most of the definitions for design were too vague because it is a process of profound thought. And like the definition, the actual design process is philosophical. Yet I believe it is important to understand the complexity and the ramification of design as it relates to restaurants. The following definition is from Wikipedia and is worth reading.

> "Design is used both as a noun and a verb. The term is often tied to the various applied arts and engineering. As a verb, "to design" refers to the process of originating and developing a plan for a product, structure, system, or component with intention. As a noun, "a design" is used for either the final (solution) plan (proposal, drawing, model, description) or the result of implementing that plan in the form of the final product of a design process. This classification aside, in its broadest sense no other limitations exist and the final product can be anything from socks and jewelry to graphical user interfaces and charts. Even virtual concepts such as corporate identity and cultural traditions such as celebration of certain holidays are sometimes designed."

For such an important concept, the question, "What is design?" appears to yield answers that have limited usefulness. Dino Dini states that the design process can be defined as "The management of constraints." He identifies two kinds of constraint: negotiable and non-negotiable. The first step in the design process is the identification, classification and selection of constraints. The process of design then proceeds from there by manipulating design variables so as to satisfy the non-negotiable constraints and optimizing those that are negotiable. It is possible for a set of non-negotiable constraints to be in conflict, resulting in a design with no solution. In this case the non-negotiable constraints must be revised. For example, take the design of a chair. A chair must support a certain weight in order to be useful, and this is a non-negotiable constraint. The cost of producing the chair might be another non-negotiable constraint, while the choice of materials and the aesthetic qualities might be negotiable.

Dino Dini theorizes that poor designs occur as a result of mismanaged constraints—something he claims can be seen in the way the video game industry makes "Must be Fun!" a negotiable constraint where he believes it should be non-negotiable.

"The design process is conflict resolution," Dino Dini states. That is very true as it pertains to restaurant design. Architects and foodservice designers are always in a process of conflict resolution, and those conflicts can involve anything from concept and vision to the size and shape of the building. If the concept is perfect, the building may be imperfect, and herein enters "cause and effect." Any constraints that exist (and there will always be some) will require conflict resolution. That is the designer's job. Whether it is a graphic designer, an interior designer or a mechanical designer, conflicts will occur. An architect might allot a block of space for the foodservice designer to design a kitchen, but the space might be too small or have other issues that could result in very poor efficiency. The foodservice designer must have the skills necessary to deal with the constraints without sacrificing efficiency or most importantly, customer experience.

Who Needs Design?

Do I need a great design team?

Every foodservice facility needs some form of design. Most need several designers, as I will explain. As you can imagine, design pertains to all aspects of your life. The clothes you wear, the map you interpret, the buildings you enter, the car you drive, the chairs you sit on and the book you read have all been designed by one or several people with purpose (and some limitations). Restaurants are no exception. A restaurant is a multi-faceted organization that requires several designers. Some are optional, and some are required. There is always some conflict between designers based on the interpretation of vision, but great designers will resolve conflicts through understanding the others' non-negotiable constraints. The end result is a restaurant that functions well and provides the ultimate customer experience. Yes, you absolutely need a great design team.

What are the objectives of a great restaurant design?

The goal is to create the ultimate customer experience, which along with profitability, is the only thing that matters. We have all been to a restaurant that's fun and beautiful but is lacking in the quality of the food. The opposite is also true. The reality is that the customer experience could have been much better. Will they come back? What if the food was great, the service was exceptional, and the atmosphere matched the concept? Will they revisit? There's no question they will, and as often as possible. The entire goal for any coffee shop or fine dining restaurant is the same—that each and every customer thoroughly enjoys their dining experience.

How can my design team achieve the ultimate customer experience?

Great design, great service, and great food are the requirements for the ultimate customer experience. To give an example, I, along with a great architectural group, lighting designer, interior designer, furniture designer and an audio/visual expert, entered into a two-month quest to create a model for the perfect restaurant. We had weeks of discussion on how to achieve that goal. The critical assignment given to each designer was to create the ultimate customer experience. To our surprise, we came unanimously to the same conclusion—that the ultimate customer experience is achieved by taking a sensory approach to restaurant design. You may think this is a bit of a stretch, but it's really not. Every great restaurant's design uses all five senses to the fullest: the sense of sight, hearing, taste, smell and touch. What is more fun than going to an Italian restaurant in which you walk in the door and immediately hear Frank Sinatra music, smell the aromas of fresh basil and garlic, see Italian Renaissance art and decor, experience the texture of the hot crusty bread, and taste the wonderful Tira Misu for dessert? If your design team has completed their tasks to near perfection, you will have already created half of the ultimate customer experience. The other half, great service and food, needs to be created by you and your staff.

How many different designers do I need?

You can choose to have several designers, or maybe you need just one or two. A lot depends on your concept, vision, and sometimes the location. Some very rural communities will not require an architect. If you are opening a small coffee shop or diner, you might decide to do the interior design on your own. In rural areas, you will generally be governed by a set of state standards. While the state, county or city is not going to be concerned with the look or flow of your facility, they will have plenty to say about code issues including health, fire, ADA codes, building, HVAC, plumbing and electrical concerns. Even if the building is pre-existing, you will still have all the code issues to address, and these have to be addressed by professionals. About 90% of all restaurants require an architect and a foodservice designer on the job. The days of hand-sketching a design are long over.

Your concept and vision may also require additional designers such as interior, lighting, audio/visual, data design, and others. These can be hired separately, or some might fall under the umbrella of the architect. In order to eliminate conflict of interest, your foodservice designer should be hired separately. As previously stated, your concept, vision and location will dictate the designers you will need. If your restaurant is in Chicago and you anticipate sales of

$5,000,000, you will want to hire the best designers available in order to create the ultimate customer experience. A big part of that customer experience happens behind the scenes, which makes restaurant design the most important aspect of any foodservice facility. It has a bearing on every aspect of the operation from beginning to end. The design process should realize your vision and utilize your space effectively—it is so much more than just the customer experience. The high cost of real-estate and labor necessitates a great design, so maximize your space with the most seating possible while creating a great flow for the kitchen and waitstaff. Reduce needless steps and save money in labor costs. Nobody can function properly without great design of the space. Site selection and design can be major budget busters if not executed to perfection. Poor design will result in extra costs for equipment, plumbing, electrical costs, HVAC, employee efficiency and seating. Add all those budget buster items together and you will end up with a poor customer experience, I guarantee it.

Do not attempt to design on your own. There are so many different code issues that change regularly. Any attempt to do so will result in immediate rejection of your plans and a great deal of wasted time and money. Your job is to carefully communicate your concept and vision to the design team. Some design features can be reduced and even eliminated depending on the size and complexity of your restaurant.

Who actually needs and requires a detailed design?

In addition to your entire staff, the city, health department, fire department, contractors, plumbers, electricians, HVAC contractors, restaurant equipment suppliers, furniture suppliers, audio/visual suppliers, point of sales system suppliers, stainless steel fabricators, and cabinet makers all require detailed designs.

Your Design Team

Choose the designers that are relevant to your concept. Each design expert is described in detail below in the order of consideration.

Architect

An architect works in the construction industry designing new buildings and the spaces around them. He/she works closely with users, clients and officials to make sure the projected designs match the needs of these groups.

Architects work on new buildings, develop groups of buildings in area regeneration projects, design alterations to existing buildings, and advise on the restoration and conservation of old properties.

On every project, architects work closely with other professionals, including engineers and surveyors to make sure their buildings meet the necessary standards. They also work closely with construction specialists on site and oversee projects from beginning to end. Architects are involved from the earliest stages of a building project—from site selection to completion.

They remain actively involved throughout each project as their ideas and plans are turned into reality. They work closely with contractors on site ensuring that works are carried out to specific standards. If any problems arise, they are quickly resolved.

Even if you are opening a small deli in an existing building, you may still be required to hire an architect. The city will require a stamped architectural plan that addresses areas of concern such as ADA codes, legal egress, occupancy loads, minimum lighting requirements and many other concerns.

There are many other design professionals that fall under the umbrella of the architect: interior design, audio/visual, data, HVAC and plumbing. You can hire a firm, or each of the required designers individually. That is your choice. A great architectural restaurant design firm will want to control all of the interior design, audio/visual and lighting, along with some of the other design requirements. They want to have complete control of the "Big Wow Factor." I recommend that you consider the architect as your source for the majority of your design with the exception of the foodservice designer. When you decide to hire your designers, however, remember that it is *your* concept and vision, not theirs. It is their job to realize and enhance your vision.

Most architects have specialties, and I highly recommend that you choose an architect that specializes in foodservice/restaurant design. They understand the complexity of a restaurant project. A residential architect likely will not have a clue about restaurant operations and generally could cost up to 20% of your budget on mistakes while greatly compromising the customer experience. Your architect must be able to work effortlessly with your foodservice consultant/restaurant designer, who will assure great flow and efficiency. A residential or office building architect will not "get it." Select an architect with the utmost scrutiny. Ask for a resume, references and a portfolio of past projects. Call their past clients and inquire about their skill, work ethic and the willingness to fully realize your concept and vision. An architect that specializes in restaurants may be a bit more expensive on the front end but will save you thousands of dollars on the back end.

Some architects only design restaurants. They are generally hired for much more than design because they create a "brand." Based on your concept and vision, they will "identify" your customers. Once there is an understanding of your customer, the architectural firm will create several names along with logos, color boards, illustrations, montages and other materials that will show you, the client, their interpretation of your vision. In short, they bring your concept and vision to a branded state. This type of architect is always hired to create a prototype that can be turned into a multi-unit operation. It's certainly something to consider.

Foodservice Consultant/Restaurant Designer (FSC)

Your FSC is the design firm that will have the most impact on your restaurant flow and efficiency. All architects, even the most experienced restaurant architect, will require a FSC.

The FSC will layout the entire space for you including seating, bar, kitchens, office space, banquet space, stages, audio/visual placement and in most cases, the restrooms. Like architects, FSCs will address all of the ADA code issues and health department concerns. In a restaurant application, your architect will create the "Big Wow Factor," while your FSC will assure flow and efficiency. What all restaurateurs need to accomplish is efficiency. A great FSC will utilize every inch of your space with the least amount of labor needed while assuring the ultimate customer experience.

Just what are the responsibilities of the foodservice consultant/restaurant designer?

- **Concept Drawing**

  This drawing is for the Business Plan as discussed in the Business Plan Instruction, and is pretty much the same drawing as the actual Foodservice Layout that is listed below. There are some differences in that the concept drawing is based on a space that does not yet exist. The main reason for the concept drawing is to put together a realistic budget for your Business Plan. The drawing enables all of the trades people and equipment suppliers to give accurate estimates of the costs. The concept drawing should be as detailed as an actual Foodservice Layout, and when the project becomes a reality, your FSC will adapt the concept drawing to the actual space. Make sure that the FSC credits most of the cost of the concept drawing into the real drawing.

- **Foodservice Layout**

  This includes seating, bar, kitchen and other spaces that are relevant to the concept and vision. Every item on the drawing will be numbered and labeled. There will also be an equipment schedule/nomenclature that corresponds with the equipment item numbers. The layout will not include smallwares or table top items, but must include even the smallest details like wall shelves, water filters, faucets, gas hoses, table mounted can openers and vital accessories. Any equipment relevant to your restaurant must be shown on the drawing for bidding and mechanical reasons. Poor FSCs will leave off some of those items and cause major mistakes prior to opening. If it is not on the drawing, it will not get priced by equipment companies and subsequently will not get ordered. Ask your prospective FSC to provide you a sample drawing set before you hire them. Look at it for the details. If you see a sink without faucets or lever drains, do not hire them. See Figure 1 on page 119 for a sample drawing.

- **Foodservice Plumbing Plan**

  This shows all the equipment and the plumbing requirements associated with that equipment. The plan shows all rough-ins, floor sinks and underground chases for beer and soda lines. The plumbing plan also addresses gas rough-ins and the BTUs required for service. These drawings must be dimensioned. The plan is accompanied by a plumbing schedule and appropriate contractor notes. See Figure 2 on page 120.

- **Foodservice Electrical Plan**

  This plan shows all the equipment and the electrical requirements associated with that equipment. The plan shows all rough-ins, amp, voltage, phase and Nema plug information. These drawings must be dimensioned also. The plan is accompanied by an electrical schedule and appropriate contractor notes. See Figure 3 on page 121.

- **Foodservice Wall Backing Plan**

  This plan is for the general contractor. There may be heavy equipment mounted to the walls in kitchens, bars and dining rooms. Wall backing is a construction function that beefs up walls in designated areas so they can handle heavy loads. Today's codes call for the majority of interior walls to be constructed with steel studs. This drawing needs to be dimensioned and accompanied with a schedule and construction notes. See Figure 4 on page 122.

- **Foodservice Equipment Elevations**

  Elevations are front and side views of all equipment. These drawings are always necessary for custom equipment and are sometimes required by the health department. A good FSC will do elevations as part of the package. Insist upon it! The elevations that are performed by exceptional FSCs will double as construction installation documents for your equipment installer. Architects will provide elevations for interior design features such as an entrance and millwork features that are decorative in nature. See Figure 5 on page 123.

- **Foodservice Finish Schedule**

  The health department will require a list of approved floor, ceiling and wall finishes in all foodservice areas. This is typically a document—not a drawing. Your architect will sometimes create the document.

- **Special Conditions Plan**

  This plan is only executed when unusual conditions exist. The FSC will isolate the special condition and provide a detail in the drawing or document.

- **Equipment Specifications**

  This is a crucial task. In order for a FSC to specify equipment properly, they must have a complete understanding of the concept, vision and menu. Each piece of equipment is selected carefully with considerations made for volume, use, budget and reliability. Your architect will require equipment specifications from your FSC. See Figure 6 on page 124.

- **Equipment Specifications Book**

  The Spec book is a complete book of the specified equipment cut sheets. A cut sheet is the manufacturer's detailed information about that equipment. On the cut sheet you will see a picture of the equipment, dimensions, plumbing and electrical information, and generally speaking, how the equipment functions. The cut sheet will also indicate the associations that have endorsed the equipment, such as NSF and UL. See Figure 7 on page 125.

- **Bid Documents**
  A good FSC will provide a bid document that corresponds to all the specified equipment and furnishing. This bid document is not for plumbers or for electrical or general contractors. The bid document refers to foodservice equipment, bar equipment and sometimes millwork and furniture. Shipping and installation are also included in the bid. Exhaust hoods could be a function of the HVAC system and may be included in the architect's bid documents. See Figure 8 on page 126.

- **Ongoing Consulting**
  FSCs are generally engaged in the design process in the very early stages, but hire one that will continue to consult and make drawing changes for you until the day of your opening. A collaborative design process always results in many changes, and you will need the cooperation of your FSC through the whole pre-opening process. Make sure their fee includes consulting and all the necessary changes until the day you are open. Any reputable FSC will want to be involved to the very end.

Foodservice consultants/designers are not required to have a specific license. There are some amazing FSCs to consider, but unfortunately, there are also bad ones. I put FSCs into two categories. One has a conflict of interest, while the other does not. They have different motives.

A FSC with a conflict of interest can pose problems, and even failure. This person is either employed by a restaurant equipment company or is a foodservice equipment specifier. Since the restaurant equipment company profits by selling you equipment, they do not always specify according to your budget. For example, they might specify needless custom equipment. In addition, instead of having professional designers on staff, they have CAD operators and sales people working up the designs—again for the purpose of selling equipment. This can not only destroy your budget by elevating your equipment costs, it might kill your flow and efficiency, and ultimately, the customer and employee experience.

A foodservice equipment specifier works basically the same way. This person is generally hired by institutional foodservice facilities such as hospitals and senior care centers. They are paid based on a percentage of equipment sales and sometimes construction costs so their practice of specifying needless custom equipment that has no useful function should come as no surprise. They are motivated by their skill at up-selling equipment and are only mildly concerned or knowledgeable about flow and efficiency. For a non-institutional venue, there is a better option.

Consider the foodservice consultant/restaurant designer that has no conflict of interest. This is a design firm in which the fee is based on a pre-determined price. Sometimes the fees are based on square footage of space, sometimes the fees are hourly, and sometimes they are determined by the complexity of the project. These FSCs do not sell equipment, nor are they on anyone's payroll other than yours. Your budget is of primary concern to the independent FSC, and they never specify equipment that does not have relevance. Their one and only motivation is to do a great job and serve the client well in order to build a relationship for repeat business.

A great restaurant designer will also save you thousands of dollars by drawing strategically. Multiple plumbing locations can absolutely break your budget, but a great designer will eliminate many of those costs. You will not get that type of service from an equipment company or specifier. With an independent FSC, you are a client, not a customer.

Are there good independent designers that have some conflict of interest? Yes, there are a few. Knowing this, as you did with architects, call their past clients and inquire about their skill, work ethic and the willingness to fully realize your concept and vision within a budget.

An architect and foodservice consultant/restaurant designer are almost always required, even on coffee shop projects. Which of these two designers should be hired first? That depends on several things. If you are purchasing property and constructing a building, you will need the architect in the very early stages. If you are renting an existing space, I suggest you bring in the FSC first. The FSC's main job is to design restaurants and foodservice facilities, and they are generally working 52 weeks a year. This is all they do. Consequently, they have had experience with great foodservice architects, but have also encountered very poor architects. Since a great FSC has developed many contacts over the years, they can help you select a qualified architect that will fit your project without exceeding your budget.

If you hire the architect first, you might be spending more money than you need to. A great FSC can minimize some of the architectural costs by providing you with the necessary drawings that nail down your concept and vision based simply on the existing square footage. In many cases, a FSC is better equipped than an architect to realize your vision due to expertise in the foodservice arena.

The architect is usually the best equipped to enlist and coordinate the necessary designers, with the exception of the FSC. The following list of designers can, and should, fall under the umbrella of an architect—or you can hire them independently.

Interior Designer

This designer is responsible for the "Big Wow Factor." The interior designer will decorate according to your concept and vision. They will develop branding, elevations and sample boards with colors, fabrics, furniture, art, lighting and signage. They get involved with every little thing that the customer can possibly see, including such things as swinging kitchen doors or banners hanging from the ceiling. If the customer could potentially see something, the interior designer will want to control it. I love working with interior designers because they can realize your interior vision to perfection. Remember the sensory theory of design? They will factor in four of the five senses: sight, hearing, touch, and smell. You will want to hire an interior designer who has restaurant experience. Your architect will want much of the control over the interior design function so I recommend that you consider your interior designer as part of the architectural team. Interior designers are not required, but if you want to create the "Big Wow Factor," it's definitely to your advantage to retain one. On the other hand, if you are developing a little café in Elephant Bute, New Mexico, you may choose to do the interior design on your own. See Figure 9 on page 127.

Audio/Visual Design

Since the explosion of the LCD television, audio/visual experts have become big players. The main focus, concept and vision of many restaurants revolves around entertainment these days. Any large venue will need experts in this field. You might have 20 or so LCD TVs, a stage, and a very elaborate karaoke and sound system. If so, you will need an expert to design the system. They will provide a wiring diagram along with equipment specifications, amp loads and rough-in locations. They will generally be under the umbrella of the architect and work closely with the FSC.

Lighting Designer

This person is generally used for very large venues. The architect, and especially the interior designers, will choose the light fixtures. The electrical designers are usually hired by the architect and will almost always provide wiring and rough-in schematics.

Mechanical Design

These designs are sometimes called "engineered drawings." They generally refer to heating, ventilation, make-up air, and air-conditioning drawings (kitchen exhaust hoods will always require an engineered mechanical drawing). Mechanical drawings are mathematical equations that relate to the balance of all the HVAC units. It gets a bit technical. These drawings can be provided by an HVAC contractor or sometimes are the function of the architect. Other mechanical drawings that may be required are: 1) plumber riser diagrams that identify water mains, waste and three-dimensional views of rough-in and pipe locations; 2) refrigeration rack drawings for large operations that are bundling remote refrigeration units onto a single refrigeration rack system; and 3) data design for P.O.S. systems, phone, internet, computer and cable connections that may be required on large projects.

The foodservice designer and architect will indicate where to locate the rough-ins, and your architect will typically handle those tasks. Electrical schematics may also be required, and will fall under the umbrella of the architect. Sprinkler systems and security systems are not always required, nor do all buildings have them. These will need some consideration, however. The complexity of all of the mechanical drawings can get a bit overwhelming. Some of the drawings are included in the contractor's work, but some are not. Your architect and FSC will point you in the right direction.

Specialty Design

This design has nothing to do with foodservice, but it might be part of the concept. Bowling alleys, arcades, dinner theaters and music venues will require specialty design. Coordinate specialty designers with your architect, FSC and other designers that are relevant to the concept.

Graphic Design

A great graphic designer will convey your vision to your clientele. Every restaurant needs signage, menus, logos, flyers, Web sites and advertising no matter the size of the space. Your graphic designer, along with your FSC and architect, is a major player in branding development. Take Mickey Mouse, for example. You instantly recognize the association to Disney. Recognition and association sells. Sport jerseys with great graphics sell, and that is true of every product that's for sale. Your graphic designer doesn't necessarily need foodservice design experience, but you will need someone who can provide the "recognition factor" by use of appealing graphics. Spend the necessary money—creative graphics will improve your sales. See Figure 10 on page 128.

Web Design

Web sites have become a marketing necessity. A large percentage of potential customers will try to gather information that will determine whether or not they should visit. A great Web site is not only an inexpensive advertising and marketing tool, but it also has the ability to create revenue through an online ordering system or merchandise sales. For consistency and branding, make your Web design the function of your graphic designer. A professional design gives you credibility and recognition in a competitive market. Also consider who will manage and regularly update your site—keeping everything current and relevant will result in more customers and revenue.

Hiring Your Design Team

If you are building from the ground up, hire your architect first, and be sure he or she has foodservice design experience. Inquire about the architect's scope of the project. Do they have a pool of all the designers necessary for the project? Make sure the foodservice consultant/ restaurant designer and graphic/web designers are hired independently from the architect. The architect should always be involved with on-site inspections and some of the construction management.

If you are renting or purchasing an existing space, you will want to consider hiring the foodservice consultant/restaurant designer first, and after that, the FSC will help you select an affordable architect who has foodservice experience. Select your design team carefully—a team whose goal it is to fulfill and even surpass your vision. I always suggest that the interior, mechanical, audio/visual and lighting designers fall under the umbrella of a foodservice architect because he can bring everyone together in a very comprehensive form. Managing all these people is stressful, and you shouldn't have to deal with it. Actually, this is the part of your project that is the most fun—where you see your concept and vision come alive. The collaboration between you and your design team can be extremely enjoyable.

The FSC will make sure your vision is accompanied by great flow and efficiency using properly specified equipment. Hire a reputable FSC that has no conflict of interest or this could completely blow your budget with facets of poor design and needless equipment. They may want leather booths when all you can afford is good vinyl booths. Of course, this can happen with any architect or interior designer, so be sure to communicate your budget constraints repeatedly, if necessary. A great foodservice architect will work within your budget, but you need to let them know what that is and stick to it.

Your location will probably dictate which designers you'll need based on code issues. If you're opening a small coffee shop or a deli in a very rural area, you may need only a FSC. But remember, even if your restaurant is in a very small town, your concept and vision must be realized by either you or your design team. If you are in a medium to large city and want to ensure profitability despite major competition, you'll want to spend the necessary funds for a great design. People go to restaurants for more than just your exceptional food. They want the total sensory dining experience. Spend your money wisely.

Fee Structure

Designers' fees vary greatly. They don't sell anything—you are paying for their creativity and expertise. Their property is intellectual in nature. You could interview two different architects who provide the same services, but one is 50% higher than the other. Maybe the designer that is higher in price is well worth it, or perhaps after checking them out, you find the cheaper of the two designers is equally or even more suitable. Interview at least two architects, FSCs and graphic designers for expertise, integrity, experience and price. Make sure they are dedicated to capturing your concept and vision.

I'm always asked if the "Big Wow Factor" created by the design team is worth the money spent. The answer is simple: "Yes!" It could easily be the difference between $1,000,000 in revenue and $2,000,000. Farfetched? No. With a great design team, you will recover your costs very quickly. If you skimp on design, your venue will be at best "ordinary," and that results in "ordinary" revenues at best.

Use the following pages to assemble the design team for your successful business.

Design Team Contacts and Information

Architect: _____

Company: _____

Address: _____

City, State, Zip: _____

Phone(s): _____

E-mail: _____

Comments: _____

_____

Foodservice Consultant/Designer: _____

Company: _____

Address: _____

City, State, Zip: _____

Phone(s): _____

E-mail: _____

Comments: _____

_____

Interior Designer: _____

Company: _____

Address: _____

City, State, Zip: _____

Phone(s): _____

E-mail: _____

Not Applicable:___ Employed by Architect:___ Employed by You:___

Comments: _____

_____

Lighting Designer: _____

Company: _____

Address: _____

City, State, Zip: _____

Phone(s): _____

E-mail: _____

Not Applicable:___ Employed by Architect:___ Employed by You:___

Comments: _____

_____

Audio/Visual Designer: _____

Company: _____

Address: _____

City, State, Zip: _____

Phone(s): _____

E-mail: _____

Not Applicable:__ Employed by Architect:__ Employed by You:__

Comments: _____
_____

Specialty Designer: _____

Company: _____

Address: _____

City, State, Zip: _____

Phone(s): _____

E-mail: _____

Not Applicable:__ Employed by Architect:__ Employed by You:__

Comments: _____
_____

Specialty Designer: _____

Company: _____

Address: _____

City, State, Zip: _____

Phone(s): _____

E-mail: _____

Not Applicable:__ Employed by Architect:__ Employed by You:__

Comments: _____
_____

Specialty Designer: _____

Company: _____

Address: _____

City, State, Zip: _____

Phone(s): _____

E-mail: _____

Not Applicable:__ Employed by Architect:__ Employed by You:__

Comments: _____
_____

Specialty Designer: _____

Company: _____

Address: _____

City, State, Zip: _____

Phone(s): _____

E-mail: _____

Not Applicable:___ Employed by Architect:___ Employed by You:___

Comments: _____
_____

Mechanical Designer: _____

Company: _____

Address: _____

City, State, Zip: _____

Phone(s): _____

E-mail: _____

Not Applicable:___ Employed by Architect:___ Employed by You:___

Comments: _____
_____

Mechanical Designer: _____

Company: _____

Address: _____

City, State, Zip: _____

Phone(s): _____

E-mail: _____

Not Applicable:___ Employed by Architect:___ Employed by You:___

Comments: _____
_____

Mechanical Designer: _____

Company: _____

Address: _____

City, State, Zip: _____

Phone(s): _____

E-mail: _____

Not Applicable:___ Employed by Architect:___ Employed by You:___

Comments: _____
_____

Mechanical Designer: _____

Company: _____

Address: _____

City, State, Zip:_____

Phone(s): _____

E-mail: _____

Not Applicable:__ Employed by Architect:__ Employed by You:__

Comments: _____

_____

Mechanical Designer: _____

Company: _____

Address: _____

City, State, Zip:_____

Phone(s): _____

E-mail: _____

Not Applicable:__ Employed by Architect:__ Employed by You:__

Comments: _____

_____

Graphic Designer: _____

Company: _____

Address: _____

City, State, Zip:_____

Phone(s): _____

E-mail: _____

Not Applicable:__ Employed by Architect:__ Employed by You:__

Comments: _____

_____

Website Designer: _____

Company: _____

Address: _____

City, State, Zip:_____

Phone(s): _____

E-mail: _____

Not Applicable:__ Employed by Architect:__ Employed by You:__

Comments: _____

_____

Other: _____

Company: _____

Address: _____

City, State, Zip:_____

Phone(s): _____

E-mail: _____

Not Applicable:__ Employed by Architect:__ Employed by You:__

Comments: _____

_____

Other: _____

Company: _____

Address: _____

City, State, Zip:_____

Phone(s): _____

E-mail: _____

Not Applicable:__ Employed by Architect:__ Employed by You:__

Comments: _____

_____

Other: _____

Company: _____

Address: _____

City, State, Zip:_____

Phone(s): _____

E-mail: _____

Not Applicable:__ Employed by Architect:__ Employed by You:__

Comments: _____

_____

Notes:_____

_____

_____

_____

_____

_____

_____

_____

_____

Samples of Foodservice Design Documents

The following documents are not to scale. These are snap shots of documents that often are quite large. The type on the snap shot will be unreadable in this scale. However, you will see some explanation added to help you better understand the documents that you will be discussing with your design team.

Figure 1 – Foodservice Layout

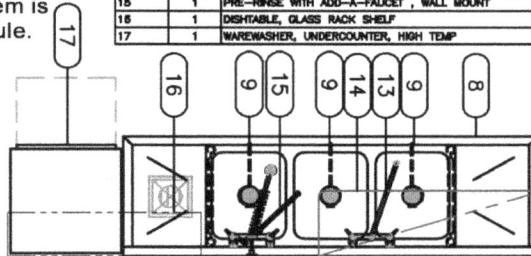

Below is a full layout of a Taco concept. Each piece of equipment on the drawing is tagged with a number. It is important that even the smallest details, such as lever drains, faucets, water filters and food processors, are on the drawing. See the blow-up section (to the right), item 8, the 3-compartment sink. You can see that each item is numbered and on the equipment schedule.

8	1	SINK, SCULLERY, 3 COMPARTMENTS
9	3	DRAINS, LEVER HANDLE
10	–	SPARE NUMBER
11	–	SPARE NUMBER
12	–	SPARE NUMBER
13	1	FAUCET, WALL MOUNT
14	2	SHELVES, WALL MOUNT
15	1	PRE–RINSE WITH ADD–A–FAUCET , WALL MOUNT
16	1	DISHTABLE, GLASS RACK SHELF
17	1	WAREWASHER, UNDERCOUNTER, HIGH TEMP

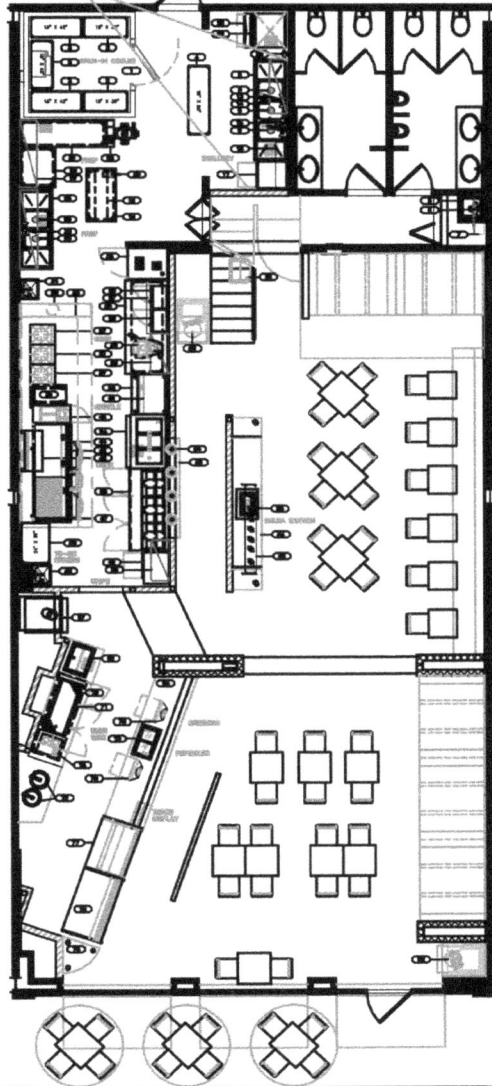

Figure 2 – Foodservice Plumbing Plan

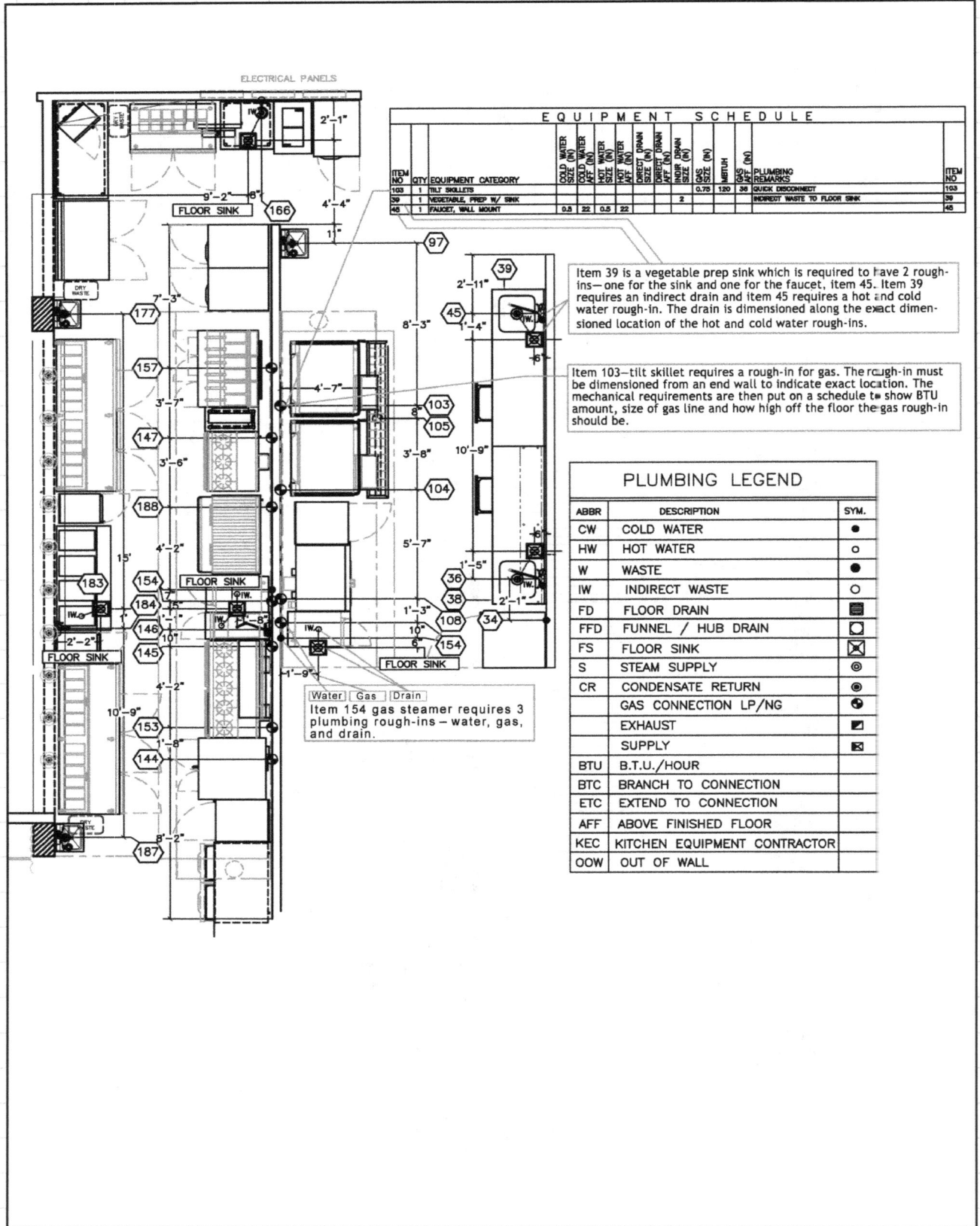

ELECTRICAL PANELS

FLOOR SINK

DRY WASTE

DRY WASTE

Item 39 is a vegetable prep sink which is required to have 2 rough-ins—one for the sink and one for the faucet, item 45. Item 39 requires an indirect drain and item 45 requires a hot and cold water rough-in. The drain is dimensioned along the exact dimensioned location of the hot and cold water rough-ins.

Item 103—tilt skillet requires a rough-in for gas. The rough-in must be dimensioned from an end wall to indicate exact location. The mechanical requirements are then put on a schedule to show BTU amount, size of gas line and how high off the floor the gas rough-in should be.

Water | Gas | Drain
Item 154 gas steamer requires 3 plumbing rough-ins – water, gas, and drain.

EQUIPMENT SCHEDULE

ITEM NO	QTY	EQUIPMENT CATEGORY	COLD WATER SIZE (IN)	COLD WATER AFF (IN)	HOT WATER SIZE (IN)	HOT WATER AFF (IN)	DIRECT DRAIN SIZE (IN)	DIRECT DRAIN AFF (IN)	INDIR DRAIN SIZE (IN)	GAS SIZE (IN)	MBTUH	GAS AFF (IN)	PLUMBING REMARKS	ITEM NO
103	1	TILT SKILLETS								0.75	120	36	QUICK DISCONNECT	103
39	1	VEGETABLE, PREP W/ SINK							2				INDIRECT WASTE TO FLOOR SINK	39
45	1	FAUCET, WALL MOUNT	0.5	22	0.5	22								45

PLUMBING LEGEND

ABBR	DESCRIPTION	SYM.
CW	COLD WATER	●
HW	HOT WATER	○
W	WASTE	●
IW	INDIRECT WASTE	○
FD	FLOOR DRAIN	▤
FFD	FUNNEL / HUB DRAIN	▢
FS	FLOOR SINK	⊠
S	STEAM SUPPLY	◎
CR	CONDENSATE RETURN	◉
	GAS CONNECTION LP/NG	⊕
	EXHAUST	◪
	SUPPLY	⊠
BTU	B.T.U./HOUR	
BTC	BRANCH TO CONNECTION	
ETC	EXTEND TO CONNECTION	
AFF	ABOVE FINISHED FLOOR	
KEC	KITCHEN EQUIPMENT CONTRACTOR	
OOW	OUT OF WALL	

Figure 3 – Foodservice Electrical Plan

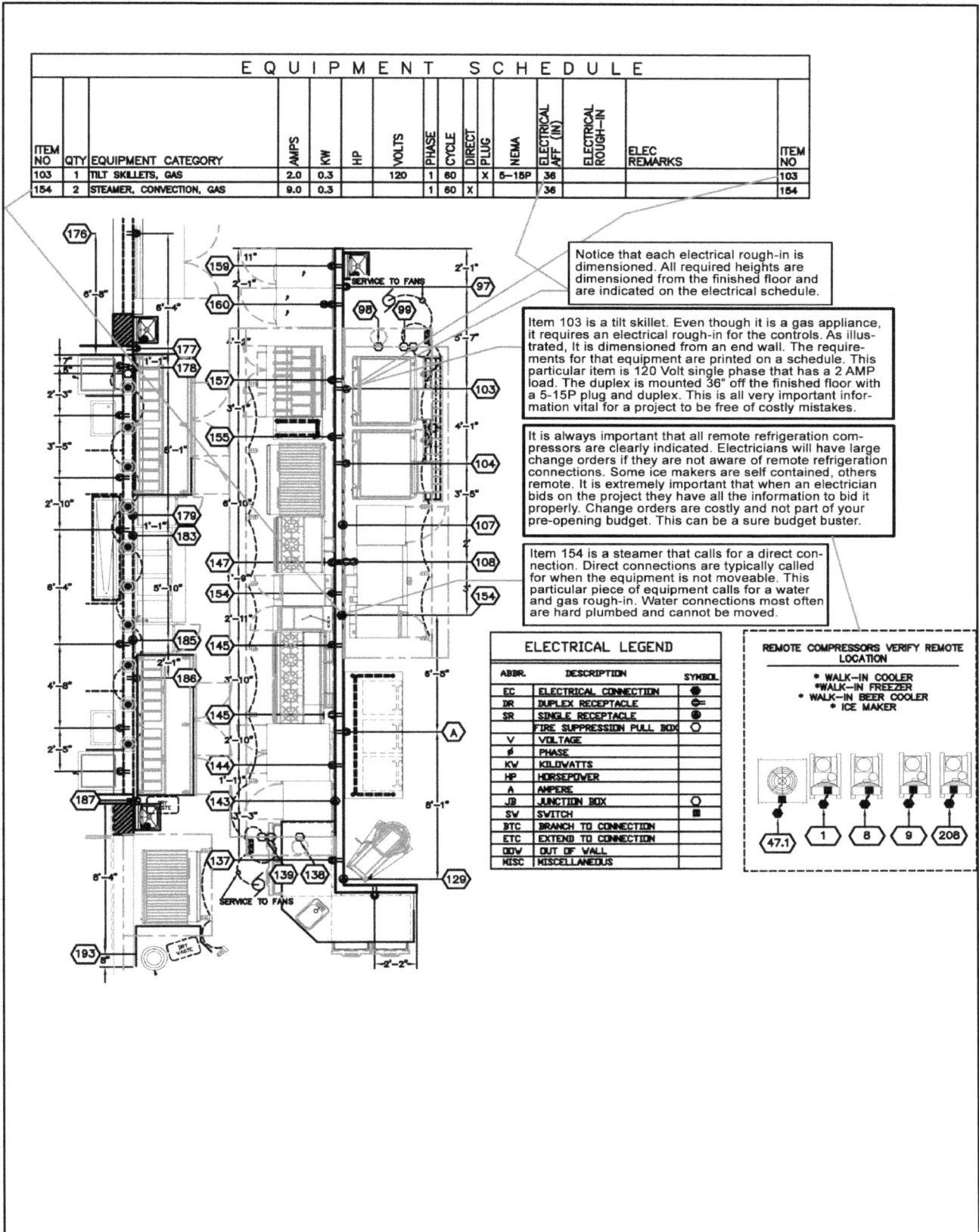

EQUIPMENT SCHEDULE

ITEM NO	QTY	EQUIPMENT CATEGORY	AMPS	KW	HP	VOLTS	PHASE	CYCLE	DIRECT	PLUG	NEMA	ELECTRICAL AFF (IN)	ELECTRICAL ROUGH-IN	ELEC REMARKS	ITEM NO
103	1	TILT SKILLETS, GAS	2.0	0.3		120	1	60	X		5-15P	36			103
154	2	STEAMER, CONVECTION, GAS	9.0	0.3			1	60	X			36			154

Notice that each electrical rough-in is dimensioned. All required heights are dimensioned from the finished floor and are indicated on the electrical schedule.

Item 103 is a tilt skillet. Even though it is a gas appliance, it requires an electrical rough-in for the controls. As illustrated, It is dimensioned from an end wall. The requirements for that equipment are printed on a schedule. This particular item is 120 Volt single phase that has a 2 AMP load. The duplex is mounted 36" off the finished floor with a 5-15P plug and duplex. This is all very important information vital for a project to be free of costly mistakes.

It is always important that all remote refrigeration compressors are clearly indicated. Electricians will have large change orders if they are not aware of remote refrigeration connections. Some ice makers are self contained, others remote. It is extremely important that when an electrician bids on the project they have all the information to bid it properly. Change orders are costly and not part of your pre-opening budget. This can be a sure budget buster.

Item 154 is a steamer that calls for a direct connection. Direct connections are typically called for when the equipment is not moveable. This particular piece of equipment calls for a water and gas rough-in. Water connections most often are hard plumbed and cannot be moved.

ELECTRICAL LEGEND

ABBR.	DESCRIPTION	SYMBOL
EC	ELECTRICAL CONNECTION	●
DR	DUPLEX RECEPTACLE	⊝
SR	SINGLE RECEPTACLE	●
	FIRE SUPPRESSION PULL BOX	○
V	VOLTAGE	
ø	PHASE	
KV	KILOWATTS	
HP	HORSEPOWER	
A	AMPERE	
JB	JUNCTION BOX	○
SW	SWITCH	▣
BTC	BRANCH TO CONNECTION	
ETC	EXTEND TO CONNECTION	
DOW	OUT OF WALL	
MISC	MISCELLANEOUS	

REMOTE COMPRESSORS VERIFY REMOTE LOCATION

* WALK-IN COOLER
*WALK-IN FREEZER
* WALK-IN BEER COOLER
* ICE MAKER

Figure 4 - Foodservice Wallbacking Plan

By definition, wall backing is material (generally plywood) inserted between wood or metal studs to add stability and structure to an area for the purpose of hanging equipment and shelves, and fastening items to a wall.

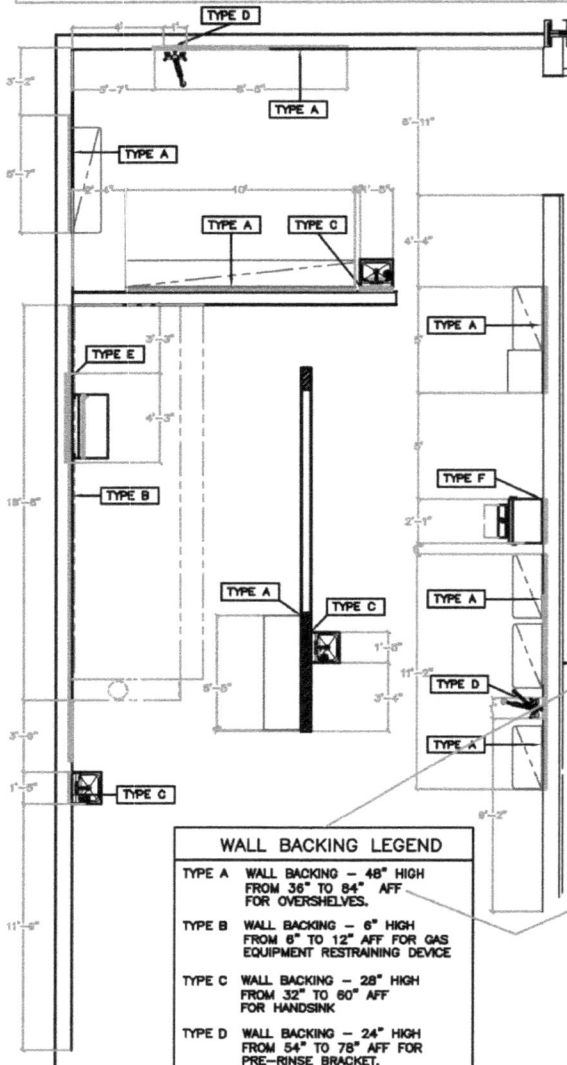

Most wall backing plans will look different. Each peice of equipment may require different wall backing sizes. In this particular plan the wall backing legend has backing A-F. Some plans will be denoted as A-R or maybe 1-7. Each designer will do it differently but with the same results. A wall backing plan is a must. If you are hanging a very heavy milk dispenser on a wall, you will need wall backing. Most commercial building codes will require non-combustible metal stud interior walls. Metal studs will not be able to support a heavy milk dispenser without the addition of wall backing.

Wall backing can be installed in between the studs or over the studs. Verify installation with the general contractor.

Wood or Metal Studs

Wall Shelves

TYPE D
TYPE A
TYPE A
TYPE A
TYPE C
TYPE A
TYPE E
TYPE B
TYPE F
TYPE A
TYPE A
TYPE C
TYPE D
TYPE A
TYPE C

Type A Backing

WALL BACKING LEGEND

TYPE A   WALL BACKING — 48" HIGH FROM 36" TO 84" AFF FOR OVERSHELVES.

TYPE B   WALL BACKING — 6" HIGH FROM 6" TO 12" AFF FOR GAS EQUIPMENT RESTRAINING DEVICE

TYPE C   WALL BACKING — 28" HIGH FROM 32" TO 60" AFF FOR HANDSINK

TYPE D   WALL BACKING — 24" HIGH FROM 54" TO 78" AFF FOR PRE-RINSE BRACKET.

TYPE E   WALL BACKING — 48" HIGH FROM 48" TO 96" AFF FOR CHEESE MELTER.

TYPE F   WALL BACKING — 48" HIGH FROM 48" TO 96" AFF FOR SALAD DISPENSER.

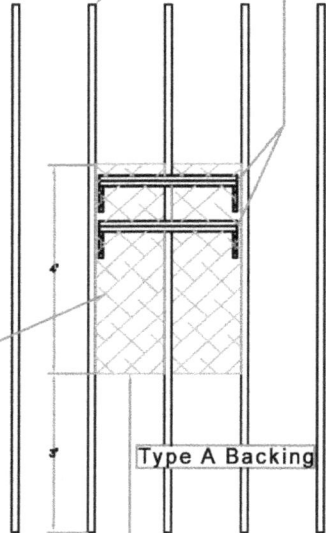

Wall backing (A) wall shelf backing is plywood 48" high. Installed 48" off the finished floor.

Figure 5 - Foodservice Equipment Elevations

Elevations are generally top and front views of equipment. There are other times when a side view is required. Side views are typically required when equipment is custom in nature. Elevations are dual purpose, the first being an actual look at a working environment and space. The other is for installation purposes. Not all designers dimension the elevations. Insist on dimensions. This is a great aid to the installers. The drawing indicates exactly where the equipment is placed and how high off the floor the equipment is installed.

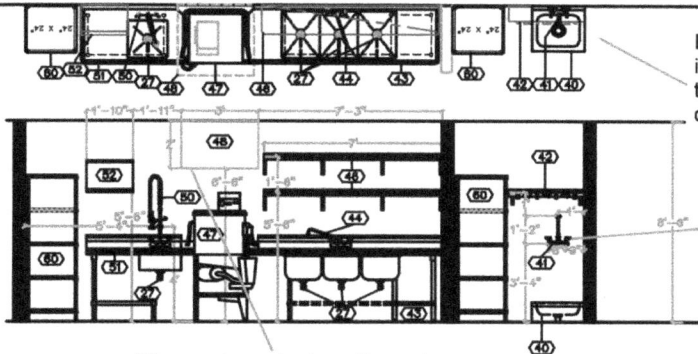

I always like to see a top view inserted with the elevation. The top view is cut from the original drawing. It is a great reference.

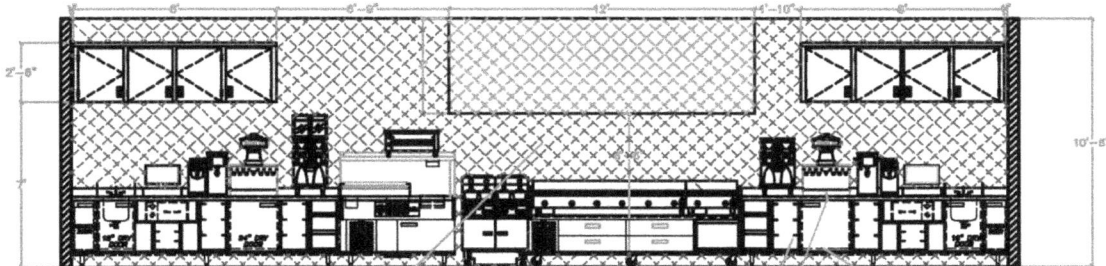

Dimensioned elevation shows how high the service sink faucet is placed off the ground.

Dimensioned elevation shows exactly where the condensate hood is located and how high off the finished floor.

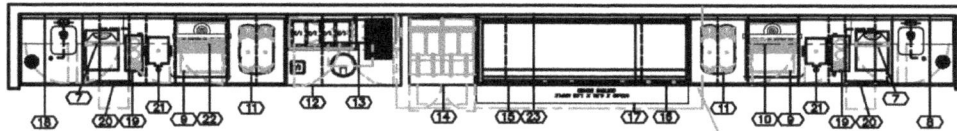

I always like to see a top view inserted with the elevation. The top view is cut from the original drawing. It is a great reference.

This elevation of Johnny Rockets is more of a decorative elevation. It indicates that a Quilted Stainless Steel Wall Panel is required. Even though it is called-out in the equipment spcification, it is always beneficial to see what it will look like.

This elevation shows such details as glass rack slides, under counter coolers and soda dispenser. This elevation will indicate the functionality of the equipment.

Figure 6 – Equipment Specifications

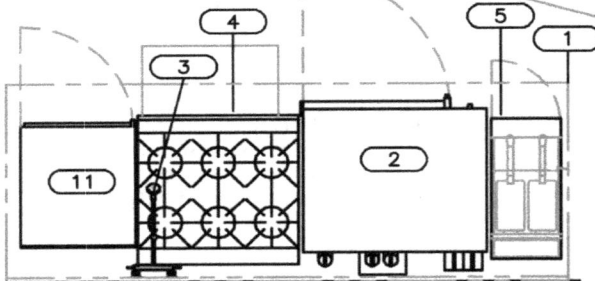

EQUIPMENT SCHEDULE

ITEM NO	QTY	EQUIPMENT CATEGORY	REMARKS
1	1	EXHAUST HOOD – 10'–6"	WITH INSULATED S.S. BACK & SIDE PANELS
2	1	OVEN—STEAMER, COMBINATION	
3	2	POT FILLER	
4	1	RANGE, HEAVY DUTY, GAS	
5	1	FRYERS, DEEP FAT, GAS	

On the drawing you will see a number on each piece of equipment. As indicated, item number 4 is a six burner range. The information that comes from a drawing is very generic in nature. The drawing does not indicate the make, model number or the required mechanical information. Your foodservice designer will furnish the information on an Auto Quotes spreadsheet along with a cut sheet showing the equipment and specifications.

SOUTHBEND

ULTIMATE RESTAURANT RANGE
36" SERIES

Configure your own custom spec sheet and model number at
www.BuildMyRange.com.
Refer to AutoQuotes for list pricing.

Standard Features
- Commercial gas range 36" wide with a 37" high cooking top
- 4" Stainless steel front rail, stainless steel front and sides
- Front located manual gas shut-off to entire range
- One year No Quibble, 24/7 parts and labor warranty
- Factory installed Regulator
- Cast iron grate top will hold a 14" stock pot
- Standing pilot for open top burners
  (Optional N/C battery spark ignition)

Optional 33K Non-clog Burners (Burner Option 1)
- (6) patented, one piece, lifetime clog free, cast iron burners
- 33,000 BTU NAT

Optional Wavy Grates (Burner Option 2)
- Cast bowl design for better efficiency
- Allows full use of entire range top
- Available only with 27K BTU Non-clog burners

Optional Cast Iron Star/Saute' Burners (Burner Option 3)
- (6) 33,000 BTU NAT star burners
- Port arrangement allows for even distribution of flame

Optional Split Burner Configuration (Burner Option 4)
- (3) Star/Saute' burners in front and (3) standard 33K burners in rear

Optional 5 Burner Configuration (Burner Options 5 and 6)
- Combine (2) Pyromax burners in the rear with either (3) standard 33K burners (Opt 5) or (3) star 33K burners (Opt 6) in the front

Optional Pyromax Burners (Burner Option 7)
- 40,000 BTU NAT
- PATENTED high output, three piece, easy clean Non-clog burner
- Built in port protection drip ring
- Group of 4 burners available

Optional Griddle Top (L or R)
- 12" (left / manual only), 24" or 36" Available
- 1 2" thick cold rolled steel griddle plate
- Manual or thermostatically controlled

Optional Charbroiler (L or R)
- 24" or 36" Available
- Removable, cast iron grates

(4361D Shown)

KI 2010 AWARD

CONSTRUCTION SPECIFICATIONS

Exterior Finish: Stainless steel front, sides and shelf standard.

RangeTop: - 27" deep cooking surface. Center-to-center measurements between burners not less than 12", side-to-side or front-to-back. A removable one piece drip tray is provided under burners to catch grease drippings.

Flue Riser: 22.5" flue riser standard with heavy duty shelf. Optional 10" and 5" flue riser available without shelf.

Oven Door: Counter balanced with heavy duty hinges.

Oven Interior: Double sided, full porcelain enamel oven cavity for superior cleanability and corrosion protection. Coved corners for easy cleaning and enhanced airflow eliminating hot/cold spots.

Legs: 6" stainless steel adjustable legs standard (casters optional)

Pressure Regulator: Factory installed.

Standard Oven Models (D)
45,000 BTU NAT oven with standing pilot and thermostat range of 175°F to 550°F (79°C to 288°C). Porcelain enamel interior measuring 14" high x 26" wide x 26.5" deep. Full sized pans fit both ways. One rack with two position side rails.

Convection Oven Models (A):
32,000 BTU NAT convection oven with standing pilot and thermostat range of 175°F to 550°F (79°C to 288°C). Porcelain enamel interior measuring 14" high x 26" wide x 24" deep. Three racks with five position side rails. 1/2 hp, 1725 rpm, 60 cycle, 115V AC, high efficiency, permanent split phase motor with permanent lubricated ball bearings, overload protection and Class "B" insulation. On/Off switch to allow CO base to operate as a standard oven.

Stainless Steel Cabinet (C)
Stainless steel cabinet base. Optional no-charge doors that open from the center.

Standard Oven with Infrared Broiler (R)
Standard Oven (see D at left), with 9,500 BTU broiler in oven.

Hybrid Electric Standard Oven (HxxxxD)
4.5kW electrically heated oven, with all the same base features of the gas standard oven at left (D)

Hybrid Electric Convection Oven (HxxxxA)
6kW electrically heated oven, with all the same base features of the gas standard oven at left (A)

Available Base Combinations
D, A, C, R, HxxxxD, HxxxxA

Form 436 Rev 4 (September/2010)

Printed in USA

Figure 7 - Equipment Spec Book

The Specification Book is required by you, your design team and government agencies. You require it to know which equipment is specified. Your design team will need it to be aware of mechanical issues, and the health department and other government agencies will need it to verify sanitation, fire and exhaust specifications. Below, you see four sheets from many that encompass a Specification Book. If the drawing schedule has 200 items on it, you will see 200 separate specification sheets that comprise a Spec Book.

Figure 8 - Bid Documents

A bid document can come in a few different forms. It might be an Auto Quotes spreadsheet, an Excel spreadsheet or Word document. The industry standard is an Auto Quotes spreadsheet. If the bid document is generated by your foodservice designer, the Auto Quotes spreadsheet or other document will indicate the item number, item, model number, quantity, specifications, and needed accessories. Each item will have an area with a line for the bidder's price. Information as in this sample will be documented.

Item– 1   Reach-in Cooler   1 each   Make– Randell   Model Number– 2010
        Electrical– 6.9 amps, .025 HP, 120 volts, 1 phase, 5-15P Nema Plug
        Accessories– 4-5" casters, 1 Bun Pan tray slides and extended warranty.
        $_____

The bid document will also include required manufacturing specifications for all custom and stainless steel items. This could include colors of materials, gauge of stainless steel, and other considerations.

SAMPLE AUTO QUOTES

nRD
National Restaurant Design

11/3/2010

Quotation

MASU

To: Masu Sushi & Robota
330 East Hennepin Avenue
Minneapolis, MN 55414

From: National Restaurant Design, Inc.

7696 209th St. N.

Forest Lake, MN 55025

Item	Qty		Description	Sell Each	Sell Total
1	1	ea	**WALK-IN COOLER**	_____	_____
			Kolpak Model No. WALK-IN COOLER		
			Walk-in Cooler, 7'6" x 12'0" x 8'6-1/4" high, backing on entire left side of cooler from 36" to 84", S/S insulated floor with Ramp, remote outdoor refrigeration system		
	1	ea	***KICKPLATES Kickplates, 36" high, diamond plate on both sides of door***	_____	_____
	1	ea	***COOLER COMPRESSOR Walk-in Cooler Remote Compressor, 3/4HP, medium temp, pre-assembled remote, air-cooled, hermetic, outdoor OP, R-404A refrigerant, 208V/1 PH compressor (7.8 amps), 120V Evaporator (2.1 amps), Head Master Controls, Medium Temp Time Clock, Adjustable Controls.***	_____	_____
	1	ea	***WARRANTY 5 Year Compressor Warranty***	_____	_____
2	1	ea	**SHELVING UNIT - WIRE**	_____	_____
			Metro Model No. SHELVING UNIT		
			Shelving Unit - Wire to consist of: (5) Shelves		
	20	ea	***1854NK3 Super Erecta® Shelf, wire, 18" W, 54" L, Metroseal 3 (corrosion-resistant) finish, plastic split sleeves are included in each carton*** 54(w) x 18(d)	_____	_____
	5	ea	***2442NK3 Super Erecta® Shelf, wire, 24" W, 42" L, Metroseal 3 (corrosion-resistant) finish, plastic split sleeves are included in each carton, with Microban® antimicrobial protection*** 42(w) x 24(d)	_____	_____
	20	ea	***86PK3 Super Erecta® SiteSelect™ Post, 86-5/8" H, adjustable leveling bolt, posts are grooved at 1" increments and numbered at 2" increments, double grooved every 8", Metroseal 3 (corrosion-resistant) finish, with Microban® antimicrobial protection*** 86.5(h)	_____	_____
3	2	ea	**BUN PAN RACK, MOBILE**	_____	_____
			Win-Holt Equipment Group Model No. ADE1820B/KDA		
			Mobile Pan Rack, full height, open sides, (20) 18"x26" pan capacity, with angle slides on 3" centers, all welded aluminum construction, end loading, 69" high, 5" polyurethane swivel casters, NSF, shipped KD 69(h) x 21(w) x 26(d)		
3OPT	2	ea	**BUN PAN RACK, MOBILE**	_____	_____

Masu Sushi & Robota

Page 1 of 20

Figure 9 - Interior Design

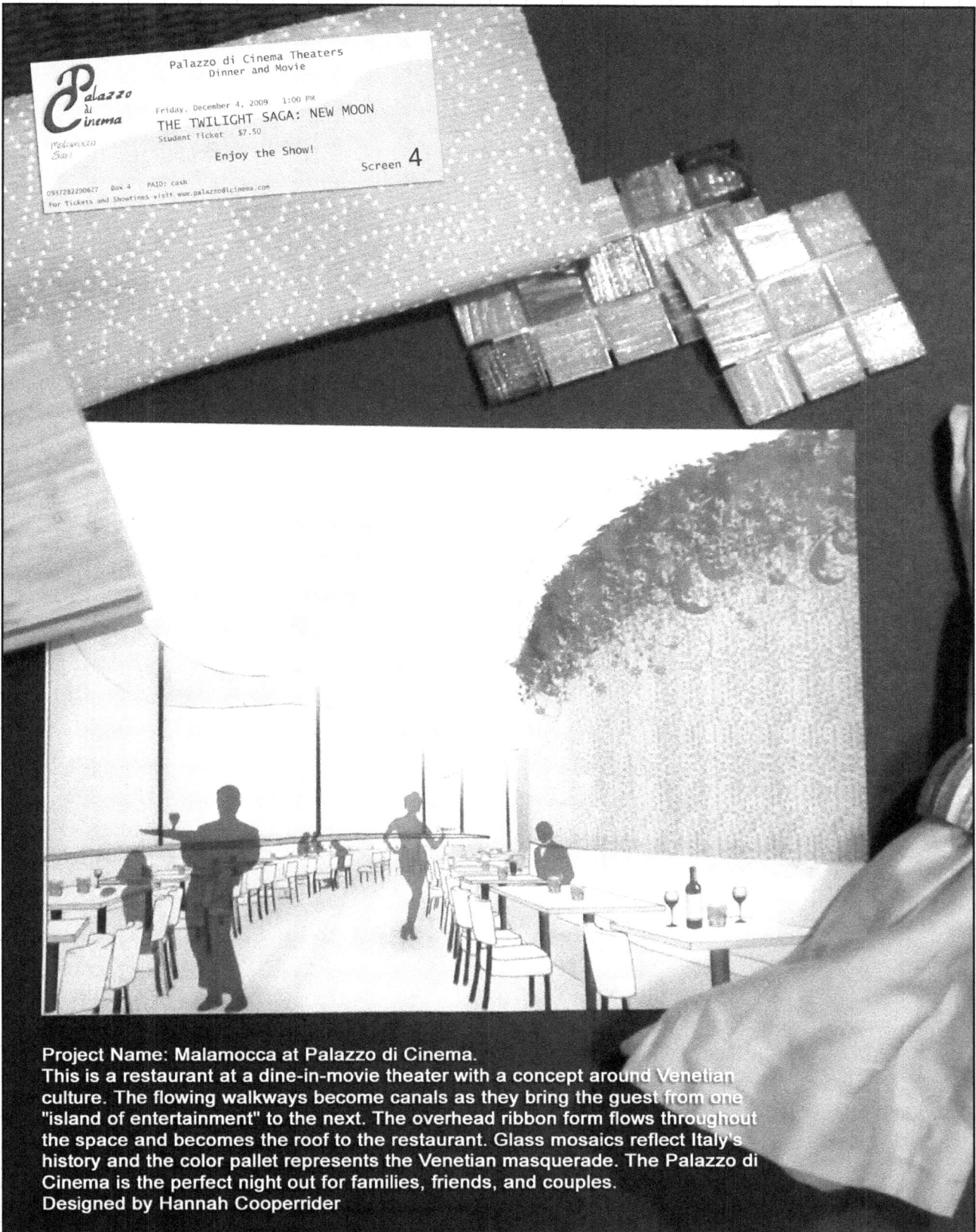

Project Name: Malamocca at Palazzo di Cinema.
This is a restaurant at a dine-in-movie theater with a concept around Venetian culture. The flowing walkways become canals as they bring the guest from one "island of entertainment" to the next. The overhead ribbon form flows throughout the space and becomes the roof to the restaurant. Glass mosaics reflect Italy's history and the color pallet represents the Venetian masquerade. The Palazzo di Cinema is the perfect night out for families, friends, and couples.
Designed by Hannah Cooperrider

Figure 10 – Graphic Design

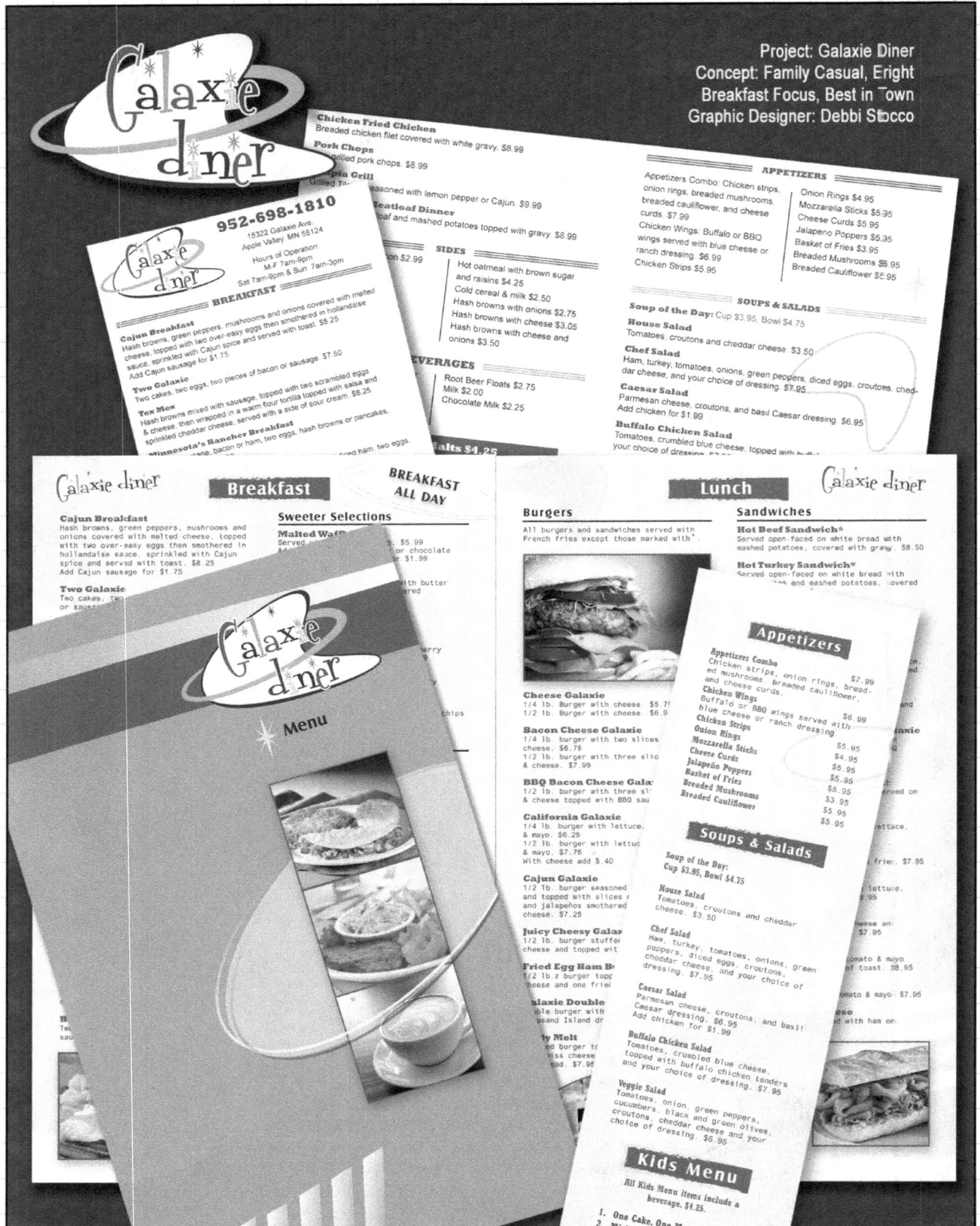

Project: Galaxie Diner
Concept: Family Casual, Eright
Breakfast Focus, Best in Town
Graphic Designer: Debbi Stocco

Notes

Instruction 7: *General Contracting*

Instruction 7: *General Contracting*

"The ultimate goal is to hire a contractor who can build to all the designer's specifications with excellence and at a reasonable price."

— FRANK STOCCO, FOODSERVICE CONSULTANT

Selecting a great contractor to build out your restaurant is one of the most important decisions you will make. Choosing the right person to suit your building and construction needs is vital to ensure that the project is completed properly, professionally, safely and on budget. There are many contractors to choose from—some specialize in residential building, others in commercial complexes, and some actually specialize in foodservice construction. You may be a do-it-yourself type of person with excellent carpentry skills, but do you know all the building codes, health department codes and ADA requirements? Do you have the time and expertise to successfully build out your restaurant while handling all of your other pre-opening responsibilities? There is always the option to be your own general contractor and hire carpenters, plumbers, electricians and other trades, but do you really want to do that? Do you have the time and expertise? I urge you concentrate on the things that will make you successful, and if your budget doesn't allow you to hire a contractor, you may want to adjust the project.

Choosing the right general contractor is not a science. In fact, it's a fairly easy and logical decision to make. The ultimate goal is to hire a contractor who can build to all the designers' specifications with excellence and at a reasonable price. Your first impulse might be to choose the cheapest one, but that's not a good plan. General contracting can be defined loosely—just like the word "automobile." You can buy a Chevy for as low as $9,000, or you can buy a Bentley for well over $100,000. Both of them will get you from Point A to Point B, but there are a hundred good reasons for the difference in price. Just like the automobile, contractors vary in quality and craftsmanship, and that makes a remarkable difference. As it applies to general contracting, cheapest is rarely the better choice. Anyone can call themselves a general contractor, but it's your job to find the one who is best qualified.

Understand Your Restaurant Build-Out

Before you hire a general contractor, you need to fully understand the scope of your restaurant project build-out. Review the following considerations in order to minimize surprises.

- If you are working with an architect, foodservice consultant/restaurant designer and the entire design team, make sure all the plans are finalized before the start of the construction project. Eliminate the unknown! Many contractors will work with architects to create a negotiated contract, so your design team will have all the detailed items that need to be priced by the general contractor. Knowing the price of each item will help you decide whether or not to keep it in the project. A good design team will offer alternatives that will result in cheaper prices without a great deal of sacrifice. For example, if you decide that a granite bar top is too expensive, your design team might suggest a laminate bar top.

- If you are not working with an architect, you may be working with a design/build contractor. These contractors design and then build your project. This is a fairly common practice in rural America, and generally applies to residential building. This method is not very practical for a restaurant, however. A general contractor is not qualified in any way, shape or form to design a fully functioning foodservice establishment.

- Understand how to read a blueprint. Do the best you can to familiarize yourself with all the little details. You have to live with the end result—your contractor does not. Besides, the more you understand, the less chance there is for cost overruns.

- Insist that your architect, FSC and design team help keep the contractor on task and within budget. Accept nothing less.

- Know your budget.

- Be extremely clear about budgets and change orders.

- Communicate an honest budget to your contractor. Do not "low ball" them because it will come back to haunt you. If you want honesty, be honest.

- Tell the contractor that un-requested change orders are not acceptable. Insist upon this! In the case of older buildings, a contractor might run into an unforeseen issue that would trigger a change order (the dreaded "can of worms" scenario). Talk to the contractor prior to hiring to get an understanding of how such an occurrence would be handled.

- Insist that you be told about all possible change orders immediately. If you do not have this in writing, you will get your final bill with $20,000 in additional charges that you did not expect. Make it clear to the contractor "in writing" that you will *not* pay for any unauthorized change orders. If you don't, I guarantee you will spend thousands of dollars and much wasted time in court. I have seen it happen too many times.

- If a change order occurs, how will you be charged? You will want to see the documented cost of that change in great detail. Contractors stand to make a lot of money on change orders so you need to be tough.

- Insist that change orders be accompanied by a documented cost with an appropriate, pre-determined mark-up. Again, do not settle for less than an agreement in writing before you do your hiring.

- Set up a pay schedule that is fair to yourself and to the contractor. Make sure the down payment is large enough to get the project going, and after that, never pay out much more than the completed work. This is hard to do, but you must protect your own interests. You don't want the job to be 25% complete with the contractor having 75% of your money. And make sure there is at least 10% due at the end of the job. The final 10% balance is retained for the purpose of a quality and quantity inspection—better known as a "punch list." Inspect the premises and check for flaws. Have the contractor correct those flaws. Review the contract with the contractor to make sure you have received everything you expected. Pay the final balance when you know all the terms of the contract have been met and that the quality of work is what was specified.

- Receive a lien waiver for every payment that is equal to the amount of money paid.

How Do I Find a Qualified General Contractor?

Like architects, general contractors have their specialties. Restaurants are a different animal—they require a contracting firm that has experience in that discipline. It's not like building a house, for example. As already stated, building, health department, ADA and fire codes will almost always require a contractor who has foodservice and restaurant experience. An unqualified contractor will absolutely bust your budget with change order after change order. That doesn't mean they're dishonest, it means they are inexperienced in restaurant build-out. Hopefully you have hired a foodservice architect and a great FSC who have endless contractor resources. In Minneapolis, for example, there are a small handful of general contractors that build-out the great majority of the foodservice facilities. They understand the scope of the project along with all the code issues. They generally understand how a restaurant needs to operate, and they eliminate change orders because of their experience. A residential builder is always a risky proposition, so use the resources of your architect and FSC. For bidding purposes, request three highly recommended contractors. The beauty of that is you will be comparing apples to apples (three highly qualified foodservice contractors all of whom are following your design team specifications). If you can have three such contractors bidding on the project, you will be able to select the least expensive one. On the other hand, if you are comparing a residential contractor to a foodservice contractor, you might be in big trouble if you choose the lowest bid.

Hopefully you will be able to obtain recommendations for three great foodservice general contractors. Then you must do the necessary research on those three in order to make an educated and logical choice. Ask for references from past restaurant build-outs. Tell them you need names, locations, phone numbers and former clients who are willing to be interviewed. Also ask for references from vendors, lumber yards, and subcontractors. If they cannot supply you with the requested references, do not consider them as a possible hire.

General Questions to Ask a General Contractor

- ❐ How long have you been in business?
- ❐ What is your restaurant build-out experience?
- ❐ What is your company's best quality?
- ❐ Is my project within the scope of your typical project?
- ❐ Are you licensed, bonded and fully insured?
- ❐ Can I have the names of at least three former clients for interviewing purposes?
- ❐ Can I have the addresses of at least three restaurants you have completed?
- ❐ Have you ever been sued by a previous client?
- ❐ Have you ever been sued by any of the subcontractors?
- ❐ Do you pay your subcontractors on time?
- ❐ Have any of your subcontractors ever placed a lien on your customer's property because you had not paid them in full?
- ❐ How often do you supply lien waivers?
- ❐ How do you price change orders?
- ❐ On average, what is the cost of change orders (an average percentage)?
- ❐ What is the process of communication you use for change orders?
- ❐ What will you do to minimize change orders?
- ❐ Who is the primary contact on the job?
- ❐ Do you complete your work on schedule?
- ❐ How much does the bid differ from the final cost (as an average percentage)?

General Questions to Ask a Reference or a Past Customer

- ☐ Was the original bid accurate? How much did it vary from the actual cost?
- ☐ Did the contractor communicate well? Were you always in the loop?
- ☐ Did they finish the job on time?
- ☐ Were they friendly to work with?
- ☐ Were they receptive to minor changes?
- ☐ How do you rate the quality of their work?
- ☐ Would you use them for your future projects?

General Questions to Ask Vendors and Subcontractors

- ☐ Does the contractor pay on time? (If the contractor does not pay the subcontractor, the subcontractor can lien your property and this results in your paying twice for the same item).
- ☐ Did the contractor communicate well with you?
- ☐ Was the contractor good at eliminating scheduling mishaps among the trade people?
- ☐ How long have you worked together?
- ☐ What do you like most about working with the contractor?
- ☐ Is there anything about the contractor you would like to see improved?

Background Check

This task is necessary for determining whether or not there are any outstanding complaints about the contractor. Make inquiries with the following offices and bureaus:

- ☐ Better Business Bureau
- ☐ State contractors
- ☐ Licensing Board
- ☐ Consumer Affairs Office
- ☐ State licensing contractor bureaus

The Construction Bidding Process

You must have completed a detailed drawing(s) and specifications before you enter into a bid process. If there are missing or vague specifications, the contractor will have an extremely hard time bidding your project. To a contractor, bad bid specifications are like a map with a missing road—a lot of guess work.

Your contractor should bid only on items that are designated by you or your architect. What follows is a list of items general contractors will typically *not* bid on.

Millwork Fabrication and Millwork Installation

I highly recommend that contractors do not produce or install cabinetry. There are NSF millwork standards to follow, and cabinet makers are best prepared to do their own install. Some contractors are educated enough to construct bar die walls, but most are not.

Kitchen Equipment Installation

In the event that you have a tiny coffee shop with just a couple of pieces of equipment, you or your contractor can choose to install them. If you are opening a typical restaurant, though, you will want your kitchen equipment provider to do the installation. They are better equipped, more experienced, and typically much cheaper than a contractor. For example, the foodservice equipment installer will uncrate the sink, assemble it, set it in the appropriate spot and level it, attach the faucet, and secure it to the wall. The contractor then makes all the final connections—his plumber connects the faucets and drains to the plumbing rough-ins. The foodservice equipment installer then caulks the sink's backsplash as required by the health department.

Furniture Installation

Tables and their bases, chairs, stools, booths and benches are installed by the company that provides them. Typically, foodservice equipment installers are required to assemble table bases and attach them to the table tops. They also are involved in uncrating chairs and stools. Like millwork, booths and benches are typically installed by the company that manufactures them. Foodservice equipment installers are normally experienced in booth installs also. Foodservice general contractors also have the experience necessary to install booths. I generally recommend that the supplier be the one to install the item.

Stainless Steel Fabrication and Installation

This installation is always a function of the foodservice equipment supplier and installer.

Exhaust Systems

There are a couple of ways to approach the exhaust system hood purchase and installation. This is a gray area—much depends on the project and circumstances. In most cases, exhaust systems are purchased and installed by the general contractor and their HVAC contractors. Foodservice equipment companies typically have the resources to sell you the exhaust hoods, exhaust fans and make-up air units and they can hire an HVAC contractor to do the installation. If your project requires additional heating and air conditioning units, I always suggest that exhaust systems fall under the umbrella of the general contractor. You never want to have two different HVAC contractors on the job. Another option is to have your foodservice equipment supplier and HVAC contractor bid on the exhaust hood, fans and make-up air. This is a common practice and will assure you that you are getting the best possible price. You will still need to have your general contractor arrange for installation though. Just keep in mind that there are timing issues among plumbing, electrical, HVAC, ceiling, carpentry, flooring and other trades people, and your general contractor will need to organize this. Generally contractors are reluctant to take any responsibility for contractors not under their hire.

Itemized Bids

All bids need to be itemized by trade. Insist upon it! Large or expensive equipment, such as exhaust hoods and make-up air units, must be itemized in the HVAC portion of the bid. The following is a typical itemized list for a restaurant construction project in a leased building. Your project may include more or fewer items. If you are purchasing land and constructing a building, the list will be much longer.

- ❏ Permits
- ❏ Demolition
- ❏ Concrete – cutting and pouring
- ❏ Framing
- ❏ Plumbing – bathroom fixtures, hot water heater, grease trap
- ❏ Electrical - fixtures
- ❏ Data lines - installation
- ❏ Audio/Visual lines – installation
- ❏ Security – the system, cameras, safes and installation
- ❏ HVAC – heating, air conditioning, ventilation, make-up air, duct work, scrubber, and duct wrap
- ❏ Drywall
- ❏ Doors
- ❏ Windows
- ❏ Painting and wall covering
- ❏ Tile
- ❏ Foodservice ceiling
- ❏ Carpeting
- ❏ Installation of millwork and foodservice equipment
- ❏ Flooring

- ❏ Painting
- ❏ Finish carpentry
- ❏ Equipment rental
- ❏ Portable restroom
- ❏ Dumpsters
- ❏ Itemized Total
- ❏ Profit and Overhead
- ❏ Grand Total

Keep in mind that each bidder's spreadsheet will be different. Make sure you request clarification if there is any little thing you do not understand. And be positively sure there are absolutely no missing or added items. Something like that could be the cause of one bid being lower than the others. Each bid must be based only on the information supplied to them by you or your architect. Let your design team help scrutinize each bid for accuracy.

Did the bids come back on budget? Whatever you do, do not blow your budget! If the bids come in over budget, you must go back to your design team and ask why. They should have designed according to your budget but you have to realize that they can't control cost increases. Make sure you allow for cost overruns as part of your building budget. If the bids come in over budget you must "value engineer." Maybe granite is out, replaced by wood. Remember, every job has some change orders. You might be able to negotiate with your contractor if it is only a few thousand dollars difference. It's the job of the design team to value engineer the project without sacrificing concept, vision and the ultimate customer experience.

Choosing a Bid

Select the best qualified and most professional contractor from the three bidders. That's common sense! The key is to get the best contractor at the best price. With three itemized bids, you will be able to understand the difference in the pricing. (Be cautious if one bid is substantially lower than the others.) The contractor you feel would do the best job for you just might be higher, but because the bid is itemized, you will be able to easily identify the areas where the bids differ. Maybe one is $2,000 higher on flooring and $3,000 higher on HVAC equipment and installation. It's your job to get the contractor to come down to the lowest bid on each item. Never show one contractor another contractor's bid—it is a very poor practice. Be honest with the person you would like to build-out your project, telling them they are priced high on flooring and HVAC and must come down on their price. It's important that your price reduction requests are communicated with the utmost respect, and that you develop a friendly and respectful relationship. If you don't, you will have a tough time opening on schedule and within your budget.

Before signing a contract, make sure all of your questions have been answered to your satisfaction. Be sure you are in agreement regarding the pay schedule, time line and lien waiver procedures. Have your architect thoroughly scrutinize the contracting bid before you proceed, just as you had the FSC scrutinize the equipment bid. For instance, most restaurateurs will not know that a roof penetration is needed for a roof-top remote refrigeration unit. Your architect and FSC will know this, and will know if anything else on the bid is missing or insufficient. It is then a good practice to have your lawyer review the contract for your financial and legal protection.

Contractor Information and References

Contractor 1: _____

Phone(s): _____

Address: _____

City:_____State:____ Zip:_____

Date of bid request: _____

Customer Reference 1:_____

Phone(s): _____

Address: _____

City:_____State:____ Zip:_____

Customer Reference 2:_____

Phone(s): _____

Address: _____

City:_____State:____ Zip:_____

Customer Reference 3:_____

Phone(s): _____

Address: _____

City:_____State:____ Zip:_____

Vendor Reference 1:_____

Phone(s): _____

Address: _____

City:_____State:____ Zip:_____

Vendor Reference 2:_____

Phone(s): _____

Address: _____

City:_____State:____ Zip:_____

Vendor Reference 3:_____

Phone(s): _____

Address: _____

City:_____State:____ Zip:_____

Notes: _____

_____

_____

_____

_____

_____

Contractor 2: _____
Phone(s): _____
Address: _____
City:_____State:____ Zip:_____
Date of bid request: _____

Customer Reference 1:_____
Phone(s): _____
Address: _____
City:_____State:____ Zip:_____
Customer Reference 2:_____
Phone(s): _____
Address: _____
City:_____State:____ Zip:_____
Customer Reference 3:_____
Phone(s): _____
Address: _____
City:_____State:____ Zip:_____

Vendor Reference 1:_____
Phone(s): _____
Address: _____
City:_____State:____ Zip:_____
Vendor Reference 2:_____
Phone(s): _____
Address: _____
City:_____State:____ Zip:_____
Vendor Reference 3:_____
Phone(s): _____
Address: _____
City:_____State:____ Zip:_____
Notes: _____
_____
_____
_____
_____
_____
_____

Contractor 3: _____

Phone(s): _____

Address: _____

City:_____State:_____ Zip:_____

Date of bid request: _____

Customer Reference 1:_____

Phone(s): _____

Address: _____

City:_____State:_____ Zip:_____

Customer Reference 2:_____

Phone(s): _____

Address: _____

City:_____State:_____ Zip:_____

Customer Reference 3:_____

Phone(s): _____

Address: _____

City:_____State:_____ Zip:_____

Vendor Reference 1:_____

Phone(s): _____

Address: _____

City:_____State:_____ Zip:_____

Vendor Reference 2:_____

Phone(s): _____

Address: _____

City:_____State:_____ Zip:_____

Vendor Reference 3:_____

Phone(s): _____

Address: _____

City:_____State:_____ Zip:_____

Notes: _____

_____

_____

_____

_____

_____

_____

_____

_____

_____

Notes

Instruction 8: Equipment Purchasing

Instruction 8: *Equipment Purchasing*

"The lowest bid does not qualify a vendor to facilitate and install the project properly. My suggestion is to always select the best qualified and most professional vendor, then get them to meet the quote of the low bidder."

— FRANK STOCCO, FOODSERVICE CONSULTANT

Before you can discuss purchasing procedures for foodservice equipment, you must have your design team's final plans. These must be accompanied by equipment specifications that include make, model numbers and all the required accessories.

Example of Equipment Specification:

Item 18
Southbend Six-Burner Range, Model # 436D
Casters
Natural Gas

Item 18.1
Dormont
Quick Disconnect Gas Hose
Model# 1675KITS48

> Items 18 and 18.1 include accessories that enable the Southbend Six-Burner Range to function properly and according to Health Department and NSF standards.

The information above is what is expected from your foodservice consultant/restaurant designer. If the line item is a custom stainless steel or millwork unit, the architect, interior designer and/or FSC must provide a detailed elevation with the specified required accessories. In the case of millwork, you need an elevation that shows possible door swings, drawers, backsplashes and finishes. Stainless steel fabrication will have the same requirements, including finishes. In the case of Johnny Rockets, they specify a quilted pattern on the stainless steel wall panels. If there are not detailed specifications, the vendors and fabricators will not be able to properly bid on your equipment package. If you have assembled a great design team according to Instruction 6, you will have a great competitive bid scenario. If not, your change order up-charges will be enormous.

Foodservice equipment includes all of the kitchen and bar equipment, side stations, and all other equipment under the guidelines of the health department. Foodservice equipment can also include millwork, furniture and exhaust systems. Instruction 8 does not include P.O.S. systems, telephone systems, computer systems, table top items, glassware, china, kitchen utensils, bar utensils or paper goods. These items will be covered later.

The purchase of equipment can involve many different vendors. It is important to understand each vendor's scope of the project and to have a competitive bid scenario. The architect, interior designer and foodservice consultant/restaurant designer should always specify equipment and furnishing that many suppliers have access to. An interior designer might specify an exotic chair and lighting fixture that very few suppliers have access to, but you must agree that the exotic chair is in your budget and would add greatly to your concept and vision. In most cases an interior designer will specify a chair that several vendors have access to so you can get a competitive price. In some very rare cases, you might able to purchase equipment directly, but a large percentage of manufacturers do not allow direct sales.

You could decide to seek out your own millwork fabricator, stainless steel fabricator, furniture suppliers, HVAC contractor for exhaust systems, and foodservice equipment suppliers from among several different suppliers. Many restaurateurs will furnish an entire kitchen using as many as five different equipment suppliers to obtain the best possible price. This is a very common practice for small projects. If your project is large, however, I do not recommend this because it's very time consuming and saves very little money. The more equipment vendors you have on the job, the more complicated the project becomes.

Mark-ups on equipment vary greatly. Typical restaurant equipment will have a lower mark-up because of the ease of comparison. Custom stainless and millwork are a bit harder to compare because they are not catalog-type items and are constructed a bit differently by each fabricator. Be aware that not all millwork and stainless steel fabricators are licensed or equipped to produce foodservice-quality equipment. The health departments throughout the country require all foodservice equipment to be fabricated by an NSF authorized vendor. There are some exceptions made for millwork fabricators but they must build to NSF standards.

Your design team will help designate the appropriate vendor for all your equipment needs. Your quest is to get the best possible prices for equipment and installation while using the least number of vendors.

Equipment Vendors

Architects

Architects do not generally supply equipment. If they are doubling as the interior designer, they may supply/sell tables, chairs, booths, benches, patio furniture, lighting fixtures, art and design accessories. Hopefully a great majority of the furnishings can also be priced by other vendors.

Interior Designers

In many cases, interior designers also supply/sell tables, chairs, booths, benches, patio furniture, lighting fixtures, art and design accessories. Hopefully you can obtain competitive pricing for a great majority of the furnishings.

General Contractor

Your general contractor may want to provide exhaust systems, and sometimes millwork and stainless steel fabrication. They are extremely proficient in organizing and facilitating exhaust systems, but millwork and stainless fabrication is typically furnished by foodservice equipment providers. Entertain pricing from your general contractor if they have fabricators that they recommend, but always get additional bids to ensure excellent competitive pricing.

Specialty Designers

Purchasing information will be supplied by lighting, audio/visual and other designers relevant to your concept and vision. Make sure the prices are accurately reflected in your budget. It's not always easy to get competitive bids on items from these designers, but they will have alternative solutions if their items do not meet your budget constraints.

Foodservice Equipment Suppliers

These vendors supply all the kitchen, bar and dining room equipment that has to meet health department and NSF standards. They are also very capable of supplying exhaust systems, millwork, stainless steel fabrication, booths, benches, tables, chairs, stools and patio furniture. Some even have sources for used equipment that will match the specifications of your design. There are different types of foodservice equipment suppliers, and some will be better for your project than others. Below you will find a description of each type. Decide which will be the best fit for your project.

- **Foodservice Contract Equipment Supplier**—supply full equipment packages for any size restaurant or foodservice facility. Foodservice contract equipment suppliers are experts in equipment specifications, millwork and stainless steel fabrication, receiving, quality inspection, assembly, equipment installation and equipment start-up. They have a full understanding of how a restaurant functions and can read a detailed blueprint of FSC equipment specifications. They can provide you with a very detailed bid—they work out of an office instead of a show room. Most restaurants over 2,000 square feet will require this type of vendor. They generally don't sell just one or two pieces of equipment, nor stock equipment in a warehouse, and they require specified lead-time to fill orders. Contract suppliers can sell smallwares and table top items, but generally would rather not. Their specialty is creating a turn-key type equipment package. If you use this type of vendor, you will be required to complete a quality inspection only at the end of the installation process.

Every major restaurant chain will use this type of equipment vendor, even small coffee shops like Starbucks. They also have limited access to used equipment, and have great relationships with leasing companies. A contract foodservice equipment supplier will create a pre-negotiated contract that consists of cost plus a percentage mark-up. They're in the same buying groups as the larger catalog equipment companies, but have more expertise and are far less expensive due to their low over-head. I highly recommend a foodservice equipment contract supplier for your restaurant equipment and furnishing— it will make your pre-opening tasks a lot easier.

Advantages: Experts in facilitating a turn-key restaurant equipment package. Excellent pricing, equipment and furnishing expertise, always have great millwork and stainless fabricators. Installation expertise, negotiated contracts, equipment start-up, warranty proficiency and professionalism. Always have a lead equipment specialist and project coordinator on every project to ensure excellent results.

Disadvantages: Require lead times on equipment purchases, not good at selling smallwares. No showroom, and typically don't stock equipment.

- **Catalog-Type Foodservice Equipment Suppliers**—vendors that can in some cases provide the same service as a contract supplier but rarely have the proficiency to do the job well. Their expertise is generally smallwares sales—not always foodservice equipment. The bulk of their sales are smallwares, table top items and kitchen replacement pieces and they are more geared to sell a few pieces of equipment at a time. Catalog-type equipment companies sell online and have large warehouses full of equipment. They stock a considerable amount and can provide next day shipping using a drop-ship method. Most of what they have is lower-end/bargain type equipment that will not perform well in high volume applications.

  If you are a small coffee shop and need a single door cooler, the catalog-type equipment supplier will be the vendor for you, although their installation skills vary. Typically they are not proficient in reading blueprints and have little expertise in facilitating the installation of larger, more complicated restaurants. They also have access to stainless and millwork fabrication. It is important to note, however, that some catalog equipment companies can provide the same expertise as a contract equipment company.

Advantages: Excellent pricing. They have catalogs, and in most cases, a show room. Next day shipping on many items. Can provide you a good level of expertise in all the same ways as a contract equipment provider in most cases.

Disadvantages: Typically do not have the expertise to fully furnish and install larger, more complicated projects. Negotiated contracts are possible, but not common. The salesperson is your equipment expert. Rarely is there a lead equipment specialist and project coordinator on every project to ensure excellent results.

- **Broad-Liners**—a company whose main function is to provide food to your establishment, and is proficient in supplying smallwares and table top items, but rarely has any expertise in selling foodservice equipment. Broad-liners will sell equipment at very low prices for the sole purpose of ensuring on-going food sales. They are not geared to equip restaurants with foodservice equipment, millwork fabrication, stainless steel fabrication, expert installation or equipment start-up.

In this company the same person who sells you a case of lettuce and frozen green beans sells and installs equipment. If you are an existing restaurant and need to replace a fryer, this may be the company for you. But if you are a new restaurant and choose to use a broad-liner to furnish and install your restaurant equipment, you will inevitably have some major problems. Remember, cheaper is not always better. You can't afford the time it takes to baby sit equipment vendors.

Advantages: Excellent pricing, and in some cases, next day shipping.

Disadvantages: Little expertise in equipment, equipment sales, installation, fabrication or start-up.

- **Used Equipment Dealers**—buy and refurbish older equipment from foodservice facilities that have closed. Used equipment comes with a very limited warranty, typically thirty days or less. Some of it is good quality, but some will break down a week after opening. The main things to keep in mind are, 1) does the equipment compromise your concept and vision, 2) will the equipment hold up to the expected volume, and 3) is the equipment equivalent to the original FSC specification? For instance, you may decide to purchase a used 10' by 30" deep three-compartment sink. Your FSC designs and specifies an 8' by 30" deep three-compartment sink. How will the larger sink fit in? The 10' sink may be a great buy, but is it worth taking the extra space or using additional hot water to fill the larger sink bowl?

Your FSC will design the perfect equipment for your concept and menu, so purchase used equipment only if it matches the size, mechanical requirements and intent of the FSC specification. It might seem like a good option for restaurateurs on a tight budget, but always consult with your FSC before purchasing—they will be able to give you the information needed for making an educated decision. And remember, the health department will require all used equipment to meet NSF standards.

Used Equipment to Avoid: Dishwashers, millwork, refrigeration, ice makers, exhaust systems, walk-in coolers, pizza conveyor ovens, six-burner ranges, fryers, discolored griddles, broilers and some (not all) stainless steel tables and stainless fabrication.

Used Equipment to Consider: Mixers, slicers, dough rollers, pizza deck ovens—any equipment that matches your FSC spec, is like new, and has an extended warranty.

Any of the vendor types detailed above might be qualified to provide you with the necessary equipment for your particular foodservice project. You may want both a contract equipment company and a catalog equipment company to bid on your equipment specifications. You will need to decide what works best for you. If you do your due diligence, you can have it all—the best possible prices, expert installation, and a professional relationship with the vendors. I'll discuss this subject further in the Bid Process Section of this Instruction, but before you are ready to choose your vendors for bidding, you need to understand the typical terminology that is used in a contract. Different vendors might use alternate terminology and breakdowns.

Terminology Used By Equipment Vendors

Auto Quotes—a program that all foodservice equipment suppliers use to provide a complete restaurant equipment quote. The program can be configured to give as much or as little information as the supplier chooses. An Auto Quotes bid shows the manufacturer of the equipment, the model number and the accessories. Each line item lists a sell price, including the sell price for each accessory. At the end of the quote you will see pricing for taxable items, freight, staging, reshipping and installation. Some vendors also break installation down into categories such as equipment, walk-in cooler, walk-in cooler refrigeration, remote refrigeration, stainless steel and millwork installation. The great thing is how easy it becomes to compare one bid to the other. Note: if you are only buying one or two pieces of equipment, you will not likely receive an Auto Quotes bid.

Freight—the cost of shipping a product from the manufacturer to your restaurant or a staging facility.

Drop-ship—shipment to your door. This is a common practice for receiving one or two pieces of equipment, but not recommended if you are furnishing a full restaurant. You may be required to take the equipment off the truck, and you will be responsible for inspecting for damage. It is almost impossible to return damaged items once the truck leaves.

Staging—a facility that is arranged and operated by your foodservice vendor. It receives and inventories all the equipment and inspects it for damage. Sometimes the staging warehouse uncrates, assembles and stores the equipment until your restaurant is ready for installation.

Re-ship—shipping from the staging facility to the restaurant site. In this case, you are not responsible for taking any equipment off the truck or inspecting the equipment for damage. That is the responsibility of the equipment vendor.

Installation—equipment assembly and placement. Walk-in coolers are installed, wall shelves are hung, millwork and stainless steel fabrication is secured, and the furniture is uncrated and set in place. Booths, tables and table bases are set in place and fastened down, if required. Some equipment will need the attention of plumbers and electricians. Once every piece of equipment is installed, back-splashes are caulked and punch list duties are performed.

Start-up—the foodservice vendor employs authorized equipment servicing agents who start and check the equipment for proper operation.

The Bidding Process

Before you can send your project out to bid, the following information has to be in a finalized stage. You need a complete set of FSC and architectural drawings that are numbered and labeled. You also need the elevations of custom equipment, stainless steel and millwork fabrications. Your architect and FSC will provide a spreadsheet with all the exact equipment specifications and all the associated accessories that correspond to the numbered and labeled drawing. Some equipment will be labeled "By Others" to designate that those items are *not* to be bid. You might be leasing a dishwasher, for example, or your soda vendor might be supplying your soda system.

Your FSC will provide you with a book of equipment cut sheets/specifications that are required by the health department and recommended to give to foodservice equipment bidders.

Choosing Bidders

Choose bidders just as carefully as you would choose a contractor. Make sure each bidder has the necessary qualifications for your particular project—do not allow anyone to bid who is not qualified. Would you hire a broad-liner company to equip a 10,000 square foot restaurant and banquet facility? I hope not.

Select three very qualified bidders, and then make sure each one follows your bid criteria. Ask for references from restaurants they have equipped, and interview the contacts for those restaurants. Keep in mind that the company who furnishes your equipment does not need to be local. If you live in a large metro area like New York City, Chicago, or L.A., you might want to consider at least one bid from a vendor in a different city. The cost of doing business in NYC, for example, is considerable and could result in a much higher bid.

Bid Criteria for Vendors

Bid Criteria #1—Bidding Format. Set strict parameters for bidding to ensure that your three bids will look almost identical. This will eliminate confusion and give you the information needed for educated discussions.

- **Pricing**

  Each number line item must show the equipment manufacturer and model number, the equipment price, accessories, model numbers of accessories, and itemized pricing of the accessory. Each line item will show the Grand Total of the equipment and accessories.

- **Freight**

  Require itemized freight costs on specific items. Typical equipment such as ranges, fryers, work tables and dishwashers can have one bulk freight cost, but ask for itemized freight costs on walk-in coolers, furniture, hoods, large ovens and other very large items that require direct shipping to the restaurant site.

- **Staging**

  The cost of staging equipment for future delivery and installation.

- **Re-Shipping**

  The cost of re-shipping the staged equipment.

- **Installation**

  Require itemized installation costs for specific items. Typical equipment such as ranges, fryers, work tables and dishwashers can have one bulk installation cost, but ask for itemized installation costs on walk-in coolers, remote refrigeration, furniture, hoods, large ovens and other very large items that may require specialized installation.

- **Start-Up**

  Request an itemized cost for this. Most vendors like to bundle this in with installation.

- **Sales Tax**

  This varies by state. Usually equipment is taxed but services, such as installation, are not.

Now that you established a bid requirement, you'll be able to compare one company to another easily. It's a little bit more work for the vendors, but if they all play by the same rules, your decision will be a slam dunk. If your three bids look completely different from one another, your valuable time will be consumed with trying to decipher them.

Bid Criteria #2—Deadlines. Establish a specific deadline for the bidding, and then request one or more weeks to review the bids after they're received. Allow bidders a day or so to fix possible mistakes. Set a date for awarding the bid.

Bid Criteria #3—Equipment Lead Times. Establish a reasonable lead time for equipment to be received. Each bidder will give you shipping date lead times, and these will all be the same because they are purchasing from the same manufacturers. Raise a question if anyone promises an unusually early lead time. Include a clause in the contract for missed shipping dates that would cause a delay in opening your restaurant.

Bid Criteria #4—Change Order Policy. Require in writing that all change orders be accompanied by a manufacturer's invoice along with a predetermined mark-up. You can get absolutely killed on change orders otherwise.

Bid Criteria #5—Payment Schedule. Each vendor will have its own payment policy, and they all vary. It is very common (and often required) that your payment be 90% complete on the day of install. Insist that the final 10% is not due until a final inspection for quantity and quality has been completed and that all found flaws have been corrected to your satisfaction. This is imperative!

Bid Criteria #6—Equipment Specifications and Substitutions. All vendors are to bid the specified equipment only, without deviation to make, model numbers and accessories. All substitutions must be presented in writing for approval by the FSC and/or owner. Any suggested substitutions must be equal or better in quality, have the same plumbing and electrical mechanical requirements, and be accompanied by the necessary accessories.

Scrutinizing Bid Specifications

By now you have three complete bids in your possession. Take your three bids and the FSC specifications and go over each line item one by one to ensure that the specifications have been followed properly. It is best to have your FSC review the specifications with you. Check the makes, model numbers and accessories for accuracy. If there are any mistakes by vendors, make notes on the vendor's line items. Contact the vendor to correct the mistakes so each bid has the same exact FSC specifications.

Scrutinizing the Bids

Once your three bids have the same exact specification information, you are ready to compare the quotes. Go through line item by line item, comparing the quotes and highlighting the lowest line item bid from each vendor. Now highlight the lowest Grand Total for each vendor. For example: Bid #1's Grand Total = $100,000; Bid #2's Grand Total = $104,000; Bid #3's Grand Total = $112,000. Now take all three bids sheets and add together each line item's "low bid" to create a fourth Grand Total. Now you will have four Grand Totals. Bid #1, Bid #2, Bid #3, and your own "low line" item bid, Bid #4. Obviously Bid #4 will be less than the Bid #1 total of $100,000.

This is a necessary exercise because you want to know the lowest possible price on each line item. Finally, take each bid, line item by line item, and put the lowest line item bid next to that item on each vendor's bid. You may find that Bid # 1 is only higher on five of the 100 separate line items. If you added up all the lowest line item bids, all three bids will be identical to Bid #4. You now have all the necessary information for negotiating the best possible equipment contract. For easy comparison, each vendor line item has their line item quote plus the lowest vendor line item quote right next to it. There is nothing unfair about this practice—you want to give yourself the best chance at the lowest possible bid.

Vendor Negotiations

Arrange a separate interview with each vendor. Indicate which items they need to bring down in price. Vendors will appreciate an opportunity to match or beat the prices of the other bidders, but never show one vendor another vendor's quote. Give each vendor a few days to revise their quote if they choose to do so.

Awarding the Contract

You selected three qualified vendors, looked at their prior work, and interviewed a few of their past customers. You received their final adjusted bids, and you are now ready to make a selection. If you have completed your due diligence, the three bids will not vary much in price—they may vary by just a couple hundred or maybe even a couple thousand dollars. This has been a long process, but by now you have built a comfort level and possibly a great relationship with one particular vendor over another. Always select the best qualified and most professional vendor. Don't base your selection exclusively on the lowest bid. What you want is the most qualified vendor at the best possible price, and one you really believe is looking out for your best interests. Big institutional bids are almost always awarded to the lowest bidder but in my opinion, the lowest bid does not qualify a vendor to facilitate and install the project properly. It's hard to put a value on expert facilitation and installation but I guarantee you that there's a big price to pay for a vendor who doesn't have their act together. Select the one that will do the best job for you so you can spend your time getting ready for opening day. Before signing the contract, make sure all deadlines can be met and that payment schedules are fully agreed upon.

Placing Your Order

Make sure you give the vendor ample time to receive, stage and assemble the equipment in the staging facility. They may require a six week lead time. Give them more than the minimum time. Manufacturers are notorious for missing deadlines.

Record the information you've gathered on vendors and their references on the next few pages.

Vendor Information and References

Vendor 1:

Company: _____

Phone(s): _____

E-mail: _____

Address: _____

City, State, Zip: _____

Date of Bid Request: _____

Customer Reference 1: _____

Phone(s): _____

E-mail: _____

Address: _____

City, State, Zip: _____

Customer Reference 2: _____

Phone(s): _____

E-mail: _____

Address: _____

City, State, Zip: _____

Customer Reference 3: _____

Phone(s): _____

E-mail: _____

Address: _____

City, State, Zip: _____

Notes: _____

_____

_____

_____

_____

_____

_____

_____

_____

Vendor 2:

Company: _____

Phone(s): _____

E-mail: _____

Address: _____

City, State, Zip:_____

Date of Bid Request: _____

Customer Reference 1:_____

Phone(s): _____

E-mail: _____

Address: _____

City, State, Zip:_____

Customer Reference 2: _____

Phone(s): _____

E-mail: _____

Address: _____

City, State, Zip:_____

Customer Reference 3: _____

Phone(s): _____

E-mail: _____

Address: _____

City, State, Zip:_____

Notes: _____

_____

_____

_____

_____

_____

_____

_____

_____

_____

_____

_____

Vendor 3:

Company: _____

Phone(s): _____

E-mail: _____

Address: _____

City, State, Zip:_____

Date of Bid Request: _____

Customer Reference 1:_____

Phone(s): _____

E-mail: _____

Address: _____

City, State, Zip:_____

Customer Reference 2: _____

Phone(s): _____

E-mail: _____

Address: _____

City, State, Zip:_____

Customer Reference 3: _____

Phone(s): _____

E-mail: _____

Address: _____

City, State, Zip:_____

Notes: _____

_____

_____

_____

_____

_____

_____

_____

_____

_____

_____

Vendor 4:

Company: _____

Phone(s): _____

E-mail: _____

Address: _____

City, State, Zip: _____

Date of Bid Request: _____

Customer Reference 1: _____

Phone(s): _____

E-mail: _____

Address: _____

City, State, Zip: _____

Customer Reference 2: _____

Phone(s): _____

E-mail: _____

Address: _____

City, State, Zip: _____

Customer Reference 3: _____

Phone(s): _____

E-mail: _____

Address: _____

City, State, Zip: _____

Notes: _____

_____

_____

_____

_____

_____

_____

_____

_____

_____

_____

Notes

Instruction 9: *Miscellaneous Equipment*

Instruction 9: *Miscellaneous Equipment*

> "Never underestimate the importance of listing and pricing out the so-called miscellaneous items that may be needed for your particular foodservice facility."
>
> — FRANK STOCCO, FOODSERVICE CONSULTANT

In Instruction 8, Equipment Purchasing, we covered how to choose the right equipment company for your restaurant at the best possible price. Some of the items covered here in Instruction 9 will require you to go through a bid process as well. We've already covered the art of bidding, so this Instruction is more of a helpful checklist of items you might need for your particular facility, that should not be overlooked. Systems like Point of Sales, computer, phone, and probably audio/visual will require you to do the necessary research to purchase the system that is perfect for your concept. If you don't do the research, you will either over- or under-estimate the power of the chosen system. For instance, if a fryer breaks down, you can replace it in a few hours, but if your P.O.S. system fails to perform as needed, you will be in real trouble.

The following checklists have many items that may or may not be relevant to your concept, or items not listed that you need. For example, bowling lanes and coin operated machines are not on this list but might be a big part of your concept. Make your own checklist of items you need to purchase, and don't count on the items in this Instruction to give you every option, variety or detail of what you need. You might see an item called Glassware, for instance, but you might not see the specific glasses you need.

I have broken these checklists into categories such as Electronics, Equipment by Room, Non-Foodservice Items, Cleaning and Maintenance Items, etc. You might need to add categories as well, in order to have a complete listing of your miscellaneous equipment needs.

Electronic Equipment

Point of Sales System

There are many Point of Sale systems in the market place that specialize in the foodservice industry. There are even P.O.S. systems that specialize in pizza delivery. The important thing is that you choose the best possible system for your concept. P.O.S systems have some pretty amazing features: inventory control, labor control, hourly sales break downs, accounting, spreadsheets, hourly labor costs, hand-held wireless, and credit card transactions. Those are only a few of the hundreds of powerful features available. It is not just a cash register! The point of all P.O.S. systems is to create a seamless ordering system that yields tight controls and vital sales information. Research the system that is appropriate for your restaurant, and if you purchase a powerful system, use it to its fullest capacity. A large percentage of restaurateurs make the mistake of purchasing a powerful system and then don't use half its features. The P.O.S. system industry has an extremely educated sales staff that can help you choose the right system for your needs. Do keep in mind, however, that they are in business to sell.

Go to other restaurants that are similar in concept to yours, and find out what they are using. Also visit show rooms and go on line. Educate yourself before you attempt to purchase a system. Typically there are several accessories for each system. For instance, you might need three ticket printers for the kitchen and the bar. Your FSC/Architect layout will help the sales person locate the appropriate stations for the printers, and they will also locate the appropriate number of monitors and cash drawers needed.

Pick the system that is right for your concept and have it priced by at least two different vendors. Make sure you have budgeted properly and be wary of over purchasing. Two systems might be made by different manufacturers but be identical in performance. The purchase price must include installation and training. The intensity of install and training will depend on the size and complexity of your project. Be aware that there may be three different costs for the system, the install and the training. P.O.S. systems are very complicated, and it is very common to have extensive pre-opening and post-opening training that can last for a week or two. Choose criteria for your system.

P.O.S. System Needs	Yes	Qty.	Notes
P.O.S. Stations			
P.O.S. Systems with Cash Drawers			
Ticket Printers			
Central Computer for P.O.S.			
Credit Card Processors (if not included with P.O.S.)			

P.O.S. System Needs	Yes	Qty.	Notes
Wireless Handheld P.O.S.			
Order Monitors			
Other:			

P.O.S. System Vendors and Characteristics

P.O.S. System Vendor 1: _____

Description of System:_____

_____

_____

_____

_____

Pre-opening training (dates): _____ N/A_____

Grand Opening training (dates): _____N/A_____

Equipment package price: $_____ Installation price: $ _____

Training price: $_____ GRAND TOTAL: $ _____

Warranties: _____

Cost of service calls: $ _____Service 7 days/week? _____

Other: _____

P.O.S. System Vendor 2: _____

Description of System:_____

_____

_____

_____

_____

Pre-opening training (dates): _____ N/A_____

Grand Opening training (dates): _____N/A_____

Equipment package price: $_____ Installation price: $ _____

Training price: $_____ GRAND TOTAL: $ _____

Warranties: _____

Cost of service calls: $ _____Service 7 days/week? _____

Other: _____

P.O.S. System Vendor 3: _____

Description of System:_____

_____

_____

_____

_____

Pre-opening training (dates): _____ N/A_____

Grand Opening training (dates): _____N/A_____

Equipment package price: $_____ Installation price: $ _____

Training price: $_____ GRAND TOTAL: $ _____

Warranties: _____

Cost of service calls: $ _____Service 7 days/week? _____

Other: _____

Again, this is a bit complicated. The above information is for reference. Doing your due diligence with this equipment need is extremely important. Do not commit to a purchase unless you are absolutely confident that the system you choose is no less than perfect for your concept. You must have complete faith in the company that is selling and servicing the equipment.

Computer System

Not every foodservice facility needs a computer, but in many cases, a computer is necessary for operating the P.O.S. system. Ask the P.O.S. provider if the computer system associated with the System can be loaded with additional software of your choosing. I recommend that all foodservice facilities have a computer. At some point you will need access to the Internet.

Computer Needs	Yes	Qty.	Notes
Computer			
Scanner			
Printer			
Recommended Software:			
Accounting			
Word Processing			
Spreadsheet			
Recommended Software:			
Graphics			
E-mail			
Other:			

Computer Needs	Yes	Qty.	Notes
Other:			

Telephone and Communication System

Simple is always better. Your FSC/Architect design will help you and the telephone sales person position the system and individual phones in the appropriate places. Your concept and business volume will dictate the number of phone lines you will need. Stay within budget—do not be oversold. Other communication systems may be necessary for your concept and volume as well. For example, you might have a large patio located a long distance from the kitchen. In that case you may want to consider a paging or two-way radio system as well.

Communication Needs	Yes	Qty.	Notes
Phone Lines			
Telephones			
Fax Line			
Fax Machines			
Wireless Hand-Held Phones			
Head Sets			
Lobby Paging System			
Waitstaff Paging System			
Two-Way Radio System			
Other:			

Security System

Security systems are typically necessary for all foodservice facilities. A good system will help promote safety and honesty. Some systems are self-contained while others are monitored by outside companies, including local police and fire departments. Consult with professionals and select the appropriate system for your needs.

Security Needs	Yes	Qty.	Notes
Cameras			
Door and Window Security			
Video Recorders			
Motion Detectors			
Links to Police and Fire Depts.			
Other:			

Audio/Visual System

If your restaurant concept has a big focus on entertainment, you will want the help of an expert so you can do it right. There are many different factors to consider in choosing the perfect system for your space, and lighting and acoustics can be a determining factor. Most components of audio/visual equipment are far beyond the average restaurateur's knowledge, so contact several designers, contractors and suppliers who specialize in this field to get competitive pricing. You may want to use a similar bidding procedure as discussed in previous Instructions. Like P.O.S. systems, installation and training are an expense that cannot be avoided. Stay faithful to your budget and be careful—audio/visual consultants will most likely over-specify. If all you need is a TV, you can purchase that at any big-box store and have your contractor install it. The architectural drawing will indicate where the reception feed and electrical outlet will be. Services for television reception and piped-in-music are quite affordable.

The audio and visual elements in your restaurant are a very important aspect of your customer's sensory experience. As stated before, the ultimate customer experience is created by using a sensory approach to design—touch, sight, sound, smell and taste. Do not minimize any of these sensory elements. A television or sound system may not be the biggest part of your concept, but that doesn't mean you should take those things lightly. Every accessory in the dining room should have an absolute purpose in helping achieve what I keep referring to as "the ultimate customer experience." Consult with your architect. They should insist on designing and controlling these components for you.

AV Needs	Yes	Qty.	Notes
Sound System for Concept			
Piped-In Music			
Intercom			
Satellite Systems			
Karaoke Systems			

AV Needs	Yes	Qty.	Notes
Televisions			
Projectors			
Satellite Reception			
Cable Reception			
Video Players			
Wi-Fi			
Other:			

Supplies by Room

The Office

Your concept and business volume may require you to have several offices: chef, manager, wine steward, banquet manager, and possibly more. Office furniture and supplies are like any other high-priced purchases so use a bidding process. Stay faithful to your budget. The following is a list of office furniture and equipment typically required by a restaurant.

Office Equipment	Yes	Qty.	Notes
Desks			
Desk Lamps			
Chairs			
Conference Tables			
File Cabinets			
Book Cases			
Wall Cabinets			
Safe			
Computers			
Printers			
Fax Machines			
Scanners			
Copiers			
Paper Shredders			
Paper Punch			

Office Equipment	Yes	Qty.	Notes
Laminator			
Paper Cutters			
Power Staplers			
Staplers			
Labeling System			
Postage Meter and Scale			
Calculators			
Telephones			
Televisions			
Projectors			
Sound System			
Bulletin Boards			
Dry Erase Markers			
Trash Cans			
Other:			

The Dining Room/Banquet Hall

Your dining room furniture will be included in your architectural and FSC drawing, but there may be items you need that will not be on their drawing. If you have an interior designer on board, most of the following will be considered. Flooring, wall and ceiling finishes were covered in preceding Instructions. These additional items may have an impact on your concept and vision. Only you and your design team will know what you need.

Dining Room/Banquet Hall	Yes	Qty.	Notes
Coat Racks			
Host Stand			
Wine Racks			
Podiums			
Portable Dance Floor			
Linens			
Vacuum Cleaners			
High Chairs			
Booster Chairs			
Service Carts			
Bussing Carts			
Raised Platforms			
Banquet Tables:			
Rectangular			
Round			
Conference Tables			
Portable Bars			
Other:			
Buffet Display			
Chafing Dishes			
Heated Shelves			
P.A. System			
Projector			
Projector Screen			
LCD Televisions			
Artwork:			

Dining Room/Banquet Hall	Yes	Qty.	Notes
Decorations:			
Other:			

The Kitchen

Not everything that belongs in the kitchen will be on your FSC drawing. For example, an inexperienced foodservice designer might not have a food processor on the drawing. The problem is it may be a heavy duty food processor that requires a 208-volt outlet and wiring, and if it's not in the drawing, it will not be wired in the area in which it is required. A great FSC will have 90% of the following items properly specified in the drawings. Your concept might require additional items as well. Your foodservice equipment supplier is always a knowledgeable source for the information you need.

Kitchen Supplies	Yes	Qty.	Notes
Food Slicer			
Food Processor			
Vegetable Cutter			
Tomato Slicer			
Lettuce Chopper			
Salad Dryer			
Meat Grinder			

Kitchen Supplies	Yes	Qty.	Notes
Buffalo Chopper			
Slot Toaster			
Conveyor Toaster			
Waffle Irons			
Rice Cooker, Table Top			
Juicer			
Beverage Dispenser			
Food Warmers, Table Top			
Mixer, Table Top			
Immersion Blender			
Portable Power Washer			
Microwave			
Heated Holding Cabinets			
Banquet Transport Cabinets			
Chafing Dishes			
Bar Blenders			
Bun Pan Racks			
Can Racks			
Dish Dollies			
Cleaning Carts			
Mop and Broom Rack			
Utility Carts			
Glass Rack Dollies			
Can Opener, Table Mount			
Can Opener, Power			
Can Crusher, Table Mount			
Can Crusher, Power			
Garbage Cans			
Recycling Bins			
Ingredient Bins			
Employee Lockers			
Ext. Door Electric Air Curtain			
Fire Extinguishers			
Mop Bucket			

Kitchen Supplies	Yes	Qty.	Notes
Other:			

Non-Disposable and Disposable Supplies

Smallwares

Smallwares are non-disposable items that every foodservice facility needs in order to operate. Your particular concept may require a thousand smallware items. Catalog Equipment suppliers and Broad-liners are the types of supplier you will want to engage in a bidding process for these items. Every reputable smallwares supplier has a pre-opening guide to assist you in smallwares selections. They also have showrooms and a sales staff with expertise in this field. Some of the items needed don't require a lot of thought, but china, glassware, silverware and table top items do. For example, don't underestimate the value of matching your china to your concept—this is a valuable part of the sensory experience. Your particular concept and vision will determine your need to get your design team involved in china, glassware and table top selection. The expense of a pre-opening smallwares package is almost always underestimated so engage two or three companies in a bidding process. Depending on the concept, your smallwares package could be as much as 10% of the equipment package. Quite often the best prices will come from the same company that will provide the bulk of your grocery items. Another important issue in selecting a smallwares supplier is inventory—the company you select will inventory all your china, silverware, glassware, etc. These items break and get lost, so you must have access to immediate delivery. Accept nothing less. Can you afford to have three extra cases of fine stemware on hand? Do you have the room to store that stemware? Those concerns are their job, not yours.

The checklist below is a sample of what is needed to operate a restaurant, bar or other food-service operation. Rely on the expertise of your smallware supplier for a pre-opening list of smallwares needed for your concept. Engage the help of your architect for table-top dishware that may impact your vision.

Typical Smallwares	Yes	Qty.	Notes
China			
Silverware			
Water Glasses			
Bar Glasses			
Salt and Pepper Shakers			
Bread Baskets			
Bar Utensils			
Pots			
Sheet Pans			
Frying Pans			
Dish Racks			
Waste Cans			
Mops			
Brooms			
Janitorial Equipment			
Other:			

Typical Smallwares	Yes	Qty.	Notes
Other:			

Paper Goods

Paper goods are typically supplied by the same company that provides your smallwares. They will have a pre-opening guide with all the paper goods that are necessary to your concept. The pre-opening package can be expensive, but stay true to your pre-opening budget. There are large mark-ups on paper goods, especially logo-printed items like cups and napkins. Again, you must require the company you select to inventory your product.

Paper Goods Products	Yes	Qty.	Notes
Napkins			
Carry-Out Products			
Toilet Paper			
Cold Cups			
Hot Cups			
Paper Towels			
Pizza Boxes			
Place Mats			
Carry-Out Bags			
Tooth Picks			
Straws			
Other:			

Paper Goods Products	Yes	Qty.	Notes
Other:			

Non-Foodservice Supplies or Services

A vast majority of restaurants use several services to supply their restaurant with items they may not have the resources to do themselves. If you were to launder your own linens, you would need a commercial washer and dryer, ironing equipment, storage, and a space large enough to house everything. Having your own laundry staff and equipment is so costly that it's typically found only in very large facilities. Like everything else in life, you don't usually do everything yourself. Some services are great cost savers. You need to find out if the services you are considering will save you time, valuable space and money or if are you better served having your staff perform some of the duties. You'll find that it makes sense to out-source some of the services that are outside you and your staff's expertise or are too labor intensive. Be sure the companies you out-source to are insured and licensed.

Linen	Yes	Qty.	Notes
Table Linens			
Waitstaff Uniforms			
Kitchen Uniforms			
Kitchen Aprons			
Kitchen Towels			
Bar Towels			
Cleaning Rags			
Other:			

Floor Rugs and Mats	Yes	Qty.	Notes
Entry Rugs			
Safety Mat (for wet areas)			
Cook's Line Mat			
Other:			

Floor Rugs and Mats	Yes	Qty.	Notes
Other:			

Cleaning

Cleaning Supplies

Many chemical companies that service the foodservice industry carry all the necessary cleaning solutions you need. A few that go hand in hand with the service are dishwasher detergents, restroom cleaning chemicals, floor mopping chemicals, kitchen sanitizer and glass cleaners. Get costs from a few different companies. They will set up a chemical station to help you control usage and eliminate waste. The cost will become significant if your employees are not trained to use the products properly, so micromanage this area. If chemical use is not controlled, you will lose a percentage point from your profits.

Cleaning Service

Restaurant cleaning services are available, and they will do as much or as little as you require: restrooms, glass, vacuuming, floor mopping, general clean-up, etc. A word of warning; this can be a big and black financial hole. Most restaurants choose to train their employees to clean and maintain their own departments. Some restaurant owners will have one or two dedicated employees do the bulk of the cleaning and other miscellaneous tasks. In most cases, they do a much better job than a cleaning service. Do the math to see if this is financially prudent or not.

Exhaust Hood and Duct Cleaning

Ductwork is part of the exhaust system. Cleaning it, and the frequency with which it must be done, is dictated by the city fire department. This big, messy job is typically completed during hours when the restaurant is closed.

Window Cleaning

Depending on the number of windows you have, this is generally a very affordable service. They will do a much better job than your employees can.

Mechanical Maintenance

This is a monthly service for checking, cleaning and maintaining foodservice equipment, refrigeration and mechanical systems. This is a good service for larger restaurants, but it is not inexpensive. You find after a year or so that they are not really fixing anything. The reason may be that they are taking very good care of the equipment and actually saving you a great deal of money in repairs. Smaller establishments will often choose to maintain the equipment themselves.

Routine Maintenance

Knife Sharpening

There are companies dedicated to sharpening all foodservice cutting equipment. They come in every week or two to replace and/or sharpen knives and other types of blades.

Fryer Grease Removal

This is the only company that actually pays you for your used materials. These companies recycle the grease and offer a small amount of money for the service. They supply you with a grease waste container and then periodically pick it up according to your usage. If you have a fryer, you will most likely be required to have this service.

Waste Removal

The size of trash containers and frequency of pick-ups will depend on the volume of your restaurant. They also supply the appropriate bins for recycling.

Indoor Plant Maintenance

Plant maintenance provides water, pruning and nutrients for your indoor plants. If you have a large number of plants and flowers, I would highly suggest you contract for this service. If not, have an employee or two who would love to have the responsibility for this.

Florist

Florists provide flowers for tables and take care of your other floral needs. Some florists are hired weekly to come in, clean the vases, and replace the old flowers with new ones.

Fryer Oil Supply

This is a relatively new service that pumps out the old fryer oil and replaces it with fresh, new oil. Some services provide pumping stations so your employees can replace oil as needed.

Co2 Supply

There are companies that supply Co2 and Co2 tanks for soda and beer systems. Sometimes these tanks are kept outside so they don't take up valuable space. In larger cities Co2 trucks are used to periodically fill the large tanks. This is a great service because you will never run out of Co2 and your employees don't have to manually change the tanks.

Outdoor Maintenance

This includes such services as landscaping, snow plowing, parking lot sweeping and maintenance of the grounds.

You can keep a list of vendors and vendor information on the following pages.

Vendor Contacts and Information

P.O.S. Vendor #1: _____
Sales Contact: _____
Phone(s): _____
Address: _____
System Manufacturer: _____
Model#: _____
Notes: _____
_____

P.O.S. Vendor #2: _____
Sales Contact: _____
Phone(s): _____
Address: _____
System Manufacturer: _____
Model#: _____
Notes: _____
_____

Computer Service Provider #1: _____
Contact Person: _____
Phone(s): _____
Address: _____
Notes: _____
_____

Computer Service Provider #2: _____
Contact Person: _____
Phone(s): _____
Address: _____
Notes: _____
_____

Communications Systems #1: _____
Contact Person: _____
Phone(s): _____
Address: _____
Notes: _____
_____

Communications Systems #2: _____

Contact Person: _____

Phone(s): _____

Address: _____

Notes: _____

Security Company #1: _____

Contact Person: _____

Phone(s): _____

Address: _____

Notes: _____

Security Company #2: _____

Contact Person: _____

Phone(s): _____

Address: _____

Notes: _____

Audio/Visual Vendor #1: _____

Contact Person: _____

Phone(s): _____

Address: _____

Notes: _____

Audio/Visual Vendor #2: _____

Contact Person: _____

Phone(s): _____

Address: _____

Notes: _____

Smallwares Vendor #1: _____

Contact Person: _____

Phone(s): _____

Address: _____

Notes: _____

Smallwares Vendor #2: _____

Contact Person: _____

Phone(s): _____

Address: _____

Notes: _____

_____

Smallwares Vendor #3: _____

Contact Person: _____

Phone(s): _____

Address: _____

Notes: _____

Smallwares Vendor #4: _____

Contact Person: _____

Phone(s): _____

Address: _____

Notes: _____

Linen Vendor: _____

Contact Person: _____

Phone(s): _____

Address: _____

Notes: _____

Rugs and Mats Vendor: _____

Contact Person: _____

Phone(s): _____

Address: _____

Notes: _____

Cleaning Supplies Vendor: _____

Contact Person: _____

Phone(s): _____

Address: _____

Notes: _____

Hood Cleaning Vendor: _____

Contact Person: _____

Phone(s): _____

Address: _____

Notes: _____

Duct Cleaning Vendor: _____

Contact Person: _____

Phone(s): _____

Address: _____

Notes: _____

_____

Window Cleaning Vendor: _____

Contact Person: _____

Phone(s): _____

Address: _____

Notes: _____

Mechanical Maintenance: _____

Contact Person: _____

Phone(s): _____

Address: _____

Notes: _____

Knife Sharpening: _____

Contact Person: _____

Phone(s): _____

Address: _____

Notes: _____

Fryer Grease Removal: _____

Contact Person: _____

Phone(s): _____

Address: _____

Notes: _____

Waste Removal: _____

Contact Person: _____

Phone(s): _____

Address: _____

Notes: _____

Fryer Oil Supply: _____

Contact Person: _____

Phone(s): _____

Address: _____

Notes: _____

Co2 Supply: _____

Contact Person: _____

Phone(s): _____

Address: _____

Notes: _____

_____

Outdoor Maintenance—Landscaping: _____

Contact Person: _____

Phone(s): _____

Address: _____

Notes: _____

Outdoor Maintenance—Snow Plowing: _____

Contact Person: _____

Phone(s): _____

Address: _____

Notes: _____

Outdoor Maintenance—Parking Lot: _____

Contact Person: _____

Phone(s): _____

Address: _____

Notes: _____

Other Vendor: _____

Function: _____

Phone(s): _____

Address: _____

Notes: _____

Other Vendor: _____

Function: _____

Phone(s): _____

Address: _____

Notes: _____

Other Vendor: _____

Function: _____

Phone(s): _____

Address: _____

Notes: _____

Other Vendor: _____

Function: _____

Phone(s): _____

Address: _____

Notes: _____

Other Vendor: _____
Function: _____
Phone(s): _____
Address: _____
Notes: _____

Other Vendor: _____
Function: _____
Phone(s): _____
Address: _____
Notes: _____

Other Vendor: _____
Function: _____
Phone(s): _____
Address: _____
Notes: _____

Other Vendor: _____
Function: _____
Phone(s): _____
Address: _____
Notes: _____

Other Vendor: _____
Function: _____
Phone(s): _____
Address: _____
Notes: _____

Other Vendor: _____
Function: _____
Phone(s): _____
Address: _____
Notes: _____

Other Vendor: _____
Function: _____
Phone(s): _____
Address: _____
Notes: _____

Instruction 10: *Policies and Procedures*

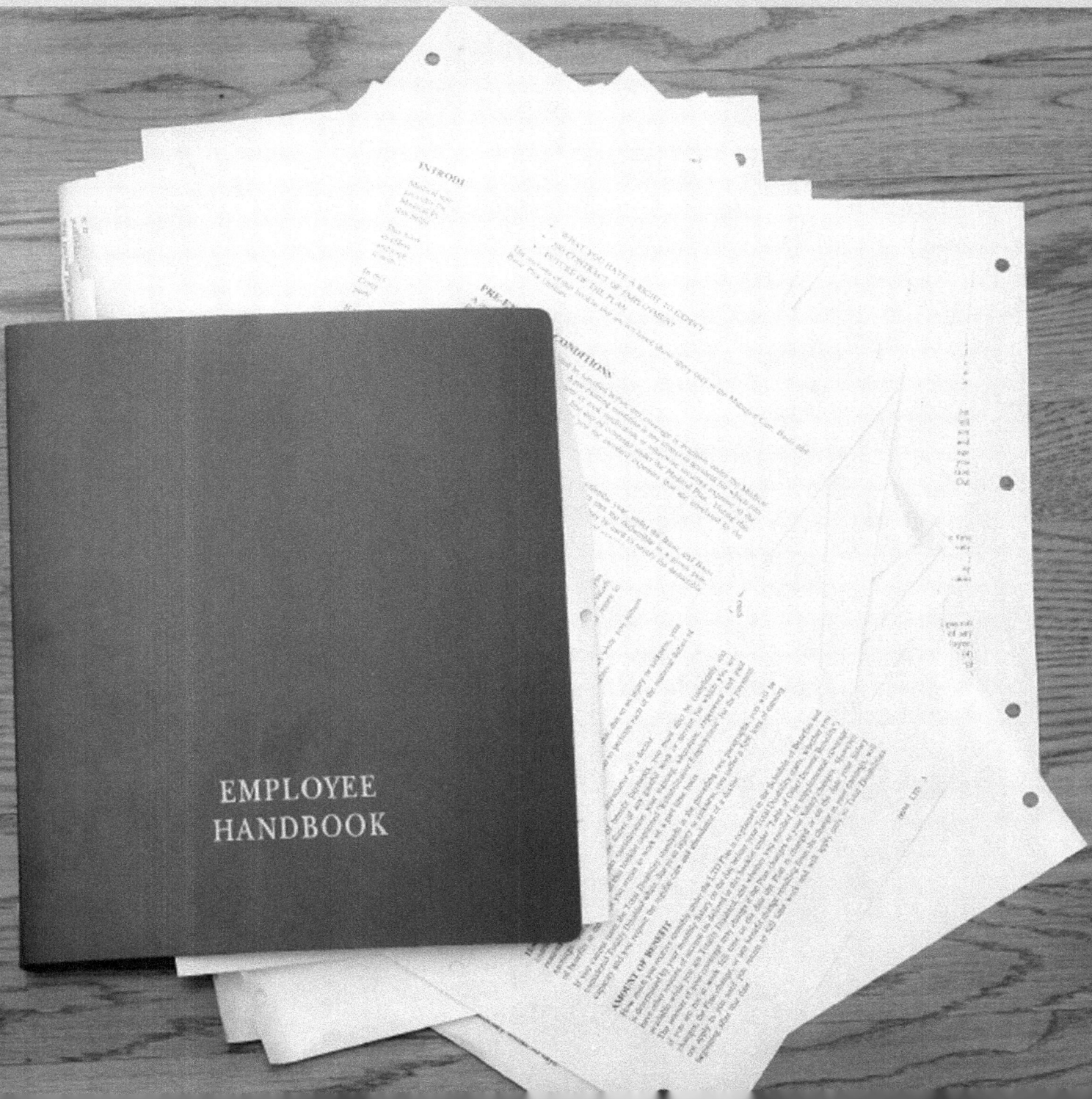

Instruction 10: *Policies and Procedures*

"Policies play a strategic role in an organization."

— WHITEEXPRESS.COM

Millions of dollars are paid out every year in the restaurant industry for sexual harassment and other legal claims. You could have a sexual harassment lawsuit brought against your company even though you had no knowledge of the incident. Did you know that you, not the perpetrator, will be named in the lawsuit? If you don't have a formal policy for reporting incidents, you could be culpable. This is just one of hundreds of policies and procedures that can cause problems if not in place and properly documented.

Policy and procedure manuals are not only designed for liability issues, but also for restaurant procedural concerns. Even if you have only one employee, you should have what most people refer to as an Employee Manual. This is a written or electronic document containing summaries of the employer's policies, procedures and benefits designed to familiarize employees with various matters affecting the employment relationship. Your employee manual should contain information that makes clear to every employee what is expected of them, what they should expect from your company, reporting procedures, and employee policies. It might also contain information for training purposes. The amount of information you put into the manual is totally up to you. The better the manual, the better chance you will have of your facility running to the best of its ability.

You may not be capable or have the expertise to create a manual of policy and procedure, but there are online programs that can be purchased for well under $100 that specialize in restaurant Employee Manuals/Handbooks. I highly recommend that you purchase one, or hire a company to help you prepare one. No matter which method you choose, you must have a lawyer that specializes in employee law review your manual.

Consider the following list of concerns. You may want to include all the topics or just a few in your particular manual. The true reason for a manual is to protect yourself and your employees by providing them with the information they need while in your employ.

What to Consider Including in the Employee Manual

Policy and Procedure Manual Inclusions	Yes	N/A
Employment Rights		
ADA; Americans with Disabilities Act		
ADEA; Age Discrimination Employment Act		
FLSA; Fair Standards Act		
FMLA; Family Medical Leave Act		
OSHA; Occupational Safety Act		
USERRA; Uniform Services Employment and Reemployment Rights Act		
At Will Employment		
Sexual Harassment		
Classification of Employees		
Drug-Free Workplace		
Equal Employment Opportunity		
Immigration Law Compliance		
Military Leave		
Discrimination		
Disability		
Pregnancy Discrimination		
Wage Garnishment		
Mandatory Breaks		
Child Labor Law		
Minor Age Employee Hour Limitations		
Non-Compete		
Employee Behavior		
Company Expectations		
Employee Expectations		
Employees as an Asset to the Company		
Business Ethics		

Policy and Procedure Manual Inclusions	Yes	N/A
Dealings with Family Members		
Dealings with Customers		
Dealings with Vendors		
Dealings with Media		
Company Property		
Employee Personal Property		
Inspection of Employee Property		
Compensation		
Computer Usage		
Confidentiality		
Conflicts of Interest		
Employee Discoveries		
Employee Suggestions		
Dress Code		
Uniforms		
Drug and Alcohol Testing		
Government Agency Inspections		
Employee Discipline		
Employee Dating and Socializing		
Employee Financial Dealings with Vendors and Customers		
Employment of Relatives		
Fiduciary Duties of Employees		
Tardiness		
Reliability		
No-Show		
E-mail Usage		
Internet Usage		
Telephone/Cell Phone Usage		
Acceptance of Gifts		
Obscene Language and Gestures		
Outside Work Activities		
Weapons		
Drug and Alcohol Consumption and Abuse		
Work Place Conduct		

Policy and Procedure Manual Inclusions	Yes	N/A
Employee Discipline		
Trademark/Copyright Infringement		
Exit Interview		
Separation of Employment		
Future References		
Employee Benefits		
Sick Leave		
Vacation		
Crime Victims Leave		
Domestic Violence Leave		
Bereavement Leave		
Employee Breaks		
Child Labor		
Adult Labor		
Meal Breaks		
Jury Duty		
Family and Medical Leave		
Employment and Re-employment		
Overtime		
Workman's Compensation		
Employee Meals		
Pay Periods		
Record Keeping		
Employee Medical Records		
Employment Records		
Employee Review of Employment Records		
Employer Withholding		
Deductions for Final Paycheck		
Promotions		
Performance Reviews		
Recording Time Worked		
Overtime		
I-9		
Work Schedules		

Policy and Procedure Manual Inclusions	Yes	N/A
Free Food		
Security and Privacy		
OSHA; Occupational Security and Health		
Employee Work Related Injuries		
Worker's Compensation		
Employee Privacy		
Opening and Closing Procedures		
Guests and Visitors		
Tours		
Non-Solicitation		
Safe Work Place		
Employee Parking		
Procedure During a Robbery		
Product Delivery Security		
Damaged Food Products		
Use of Company Proprietary Information		
Cash Control		
Tip Reporting		
Minimum Tip Rate Determination Agreement		
Cash Register Policies		
Customer Refunds		
Free Food		
Skimming Excess Cash		
Deposits		
Locks, Keys and Safe Combinations		
Security Codes and Passwords		
Customer Service		
Alcoholic Beverages		
Food Handling Procedures		
Sanitation		
Employee Hand Washing		
Hand Gel Use		
Equipment Cleaning and Sanitizing		
Food Safety		

Policy and Procedure Manual Inclusions	Yes	N/A
Food Safety Certification		
Employees and Food Safety Training		
Maintaining Food Temperatures		
Approved Vendors for Food and Beverages		
Pest Control		
Poisonous and Toxic Materials		
Food Security		
Food Terrorism		
Food Recall		
Other:		

I know this seems like a lot of topics to cover. That is why I suggest using a computer program that will develop and organize the manual. Some of the software programs are so comprehensive that it just requires you to answer simple questions. Again, have a lawyer with labor law experience review the manual when you're done.

A great Employee Manual will aid both you and your employees. Fewer questions on procedures will be asked and employer/employee expectations will never be in question.

Notes

Instruction 11: *Employee Hiring*

Instruction 11: *Employee Hiring*

"Remember, your restaurant has entertainment value and your employees are the performers. They must perform flawlessly in order to achieve the ultimate customer experience."

— FRANK STOCCO, FOODSERVICE CONSULTANT

You may already have hired several key employees if their participation is needed for all the pre-opening tasks and procedures (key personnel procurement). Your chef will have designed the menu and completed the necessary research and development. He or she would also have established your food suppliers and possibly may have hired a key employee such as a Sous Chef. This will be true of many of the department heads that are part of your management team. One of the most important jobs of those department heads is hiring a qualified staff that they will manage. Who is more qualified to hire a kitchen staff than your Executive Chef? To use an example, the owner of the Chicago Cubs hires a general manager who then hires a field manager. The field manager hires the coaches that best fit the system. Restaurants function the same way. An owner may not be qualified to hire a Sous Chef. Your department heads are equipped to hire the personnel that best fit with the overall philosophies of your concept and vision. If you are a very small establishment and don't have key personnel to do the pre-hires, you will do all the hiring on your own.

As discussed in the previous Instruction, I highly suggest that your company policy and procedure manual be completed before you begin hiring. Your prospective employees need to have clear and concise information so they are aware of all the policies, procedures and the general expectations.

Restaurants and foodservice venues have always had a large turnover in employees. Employee recruiting and training becomes an ongoing challenge for department heads. The first group of employees you hire is always the biggest challenge. The department heads are the only staff who have full knowledge of your concept and vision, and that puts a lot of pressure on everyone. Once you have opened and become established, hiring employees and training them becomes less stressful. Of all the pre-opening procedures, hiring employees may be the most important. Restaurants, unlike other industries, are very busy from day number one so it's imperative that the staff is ready for the onslaught of business. The honeymoon period will be short.

Employee qualifications vary with each position. Some will require prior experience, others will not. The more an applicant has performed the job they are applying for, the easier it will be to get good results right away. Be leery of job jumpers—they will not stay long. There is no such thing as a typical restaurant industry employee—they come from all segments of society. There are actors, accountants, lawyers, artists and others that join the foodservice industry to supplement their income while working toward something different. In any restaurant you will find employees with masters degrees and employees that have not finished high school. This makes the foodservice industry employee as diverse as they come. That's a good thing, as it's one of the things that make restaurants interesting to customers. I believe in having a good mixture of experienced employees and employees new to the industry, and I urge you to incorporate this into your concept.

When opening a new restaurant, your experienced employees need to have the character and patience to work in a very hectic environment for as long as it takes to develop a fully functioning staff. Character matters! One difficult employee can have a catastrophic influence on every other employee, resulting in complete chaos or even moral corruption. And that corruption will eventually trickle down to the customer experience. Does this sound overstated? Trust me, it is not. Hire people with character.

We have talked about the ultimate customer experience, but it's also your job to create the ultimate *employee* experience. Create a safe working environment for all. A lot of your employees will be young and easily influenced by older employees. Your restaurant will always be an attractive place to work if Joe Smith feels comfortable that his son or daughter is working in a safe environment. Foodservice qualifications are never more important than character qualifications, so never hire someone on the spot. Spend at least 20 minutes with an applicant asking general questions. If you like their qualifications and personality, invite them back for a second interview and spend some time discussing character issues.

There are many great books on the market that specialize in employee hiring and relations, and I urge you to purchase one. Employees with good work ethic and character are going to result in what every owner is looking for—the ultimate customer experience.

Employee Hiring Tips

- ❏ Create application forms. You can purchase these or design them for your specific needs. You might want different applications for each job category but this is not necessary in most cases.

- ❏ Set up specific dates and times for employee hiring. This enables your staff to be fully prepared and focused on the task at hand. Schedule at least 15 minutes of interview time with each applicant. In large venues, designate a person to schedule interviews with department heads.

- ❏ Use multiple media resources to attract applicants: print ads, Internet, word of mouth, hand-distributed business cards, and signage.

- ❏ Have personal knowledge of each position for which you are hiring. Employees should be self motivated, extremely personable, and intelligent. Remember, your employee needs the capability to present and sell your product.

- ❏ Be patient enough to get the right person for the job. Do not hire someone just to fill a position. Make sure they fit all the required criteria and are fully qualified.

- ❏ Prepare a list of character-related questions that will help you make comparisons. Ask each applicant how they react in stressful situations, for example. If all the prospective applicants are asked the same set of questions, you will be able to better evaluate their character by their responses.

- ❏ Prepare a list of skill questions for each department. Ask cooks and waitstaff different questions. Their answers will help you evaluate their skill set.

- ❏ Conduct at least two interviews before hiring. The second interview is much more in depth than the first. Make sure the applicant has the character and skill-set to properly represent your company.

- ❏ Rate the prospects on a scale of 1 to 10 in two separate categories: character and skills. Set a minimum rating number for hiring requirements. I would consider setting the bar at 10. This system will prevent you from hiring an extremely talented person with obvious character flaws.

- ❏ Make sure you allow plenty of time for hiring. If you rush, your selection of employees will show poor results.

- ❏ Present each new hire with a policy and procedure manual. Include a signature page that indicates they have carefully read and understand all the employer/employee expectations. Ask each new employee a few questions about the manual so you are assured they understand what is expected of them.

Hire the right employees for your restaurant. Your standards and expectations should be high. Lead by example. If you lack character, your employees will inevitably follow suit. Your employees are what makes your concept and vision work, so hire people who are intelligent and fun. Remember, your restaurant has entertainment value and your employees are the performers. They must perform flawlessly in order to achieve the ultimate customer experience.

Employee Positions for a Typical Restaurant

Each foodservice establishment will have different employees. Coffee shops will not need cooks or waitstaff, for example. The following is a general list of positions in a typical establishment. The positions in bold are possible early hires. Use this checklist to determine the employment needed specific to your venue.

Position	How Many?	N/A
Executive Chef		
Sous Chef		
Line Cooks		
Prep Cooks		
Banquet Chef		
Baker		
Pantry		
Dishwashers		
Maintenance		
Other:		
Dining Room Manager		
Waitstaff		
Bussers		
Counter Servers		
Cashiers		
Hosts		
Other:		

Position	How Many?	N/A
Bar Manager		
Wine Steward		
Bartenders		
Bar Backs		
Barista		
Other:		
Food and Beverage Director		
General Manager		
Assistant Manager		
Banquet Manager		
Office Manager		
Controller		
Human Resources Manager		
Other:		

Notes

Instruction 12: *Employee Training*

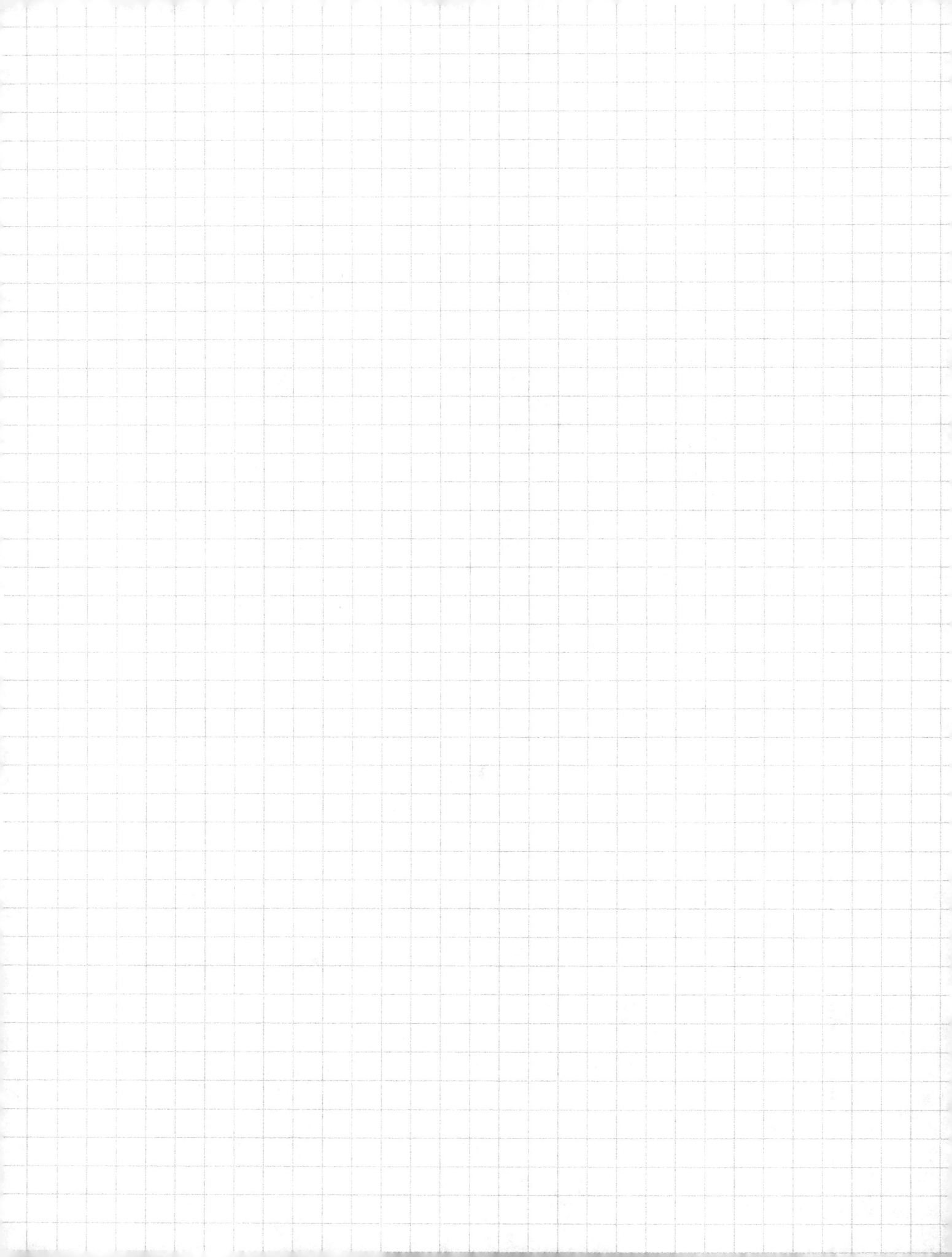

Instruction 12: *Employee Training*

"The ultimate customer experience can be realized from the first meal served if your staff has been properly trained."

— Frank Stocco, Foodservice Consultant

Can your restaurant get outstanding reviews from the time the first meal is served? Customers will determine how successful your restaurant will become beginning the day you open. I have a tendency to wait for at least two weeks before I dine at a new restaurant. By then the staff is up to speed and the systems are running pretty well. By then I am getting the value I expect— great food and great service. However, waiting a couple of weeks is not the norm. The typical patron will not wait—they want to be the first customer in that exciting new restaurant you are opening. Do they know the first couple of weeks are a challenge? I believe most do, and they will afford you some grace. Most customers will accept one bad experience because they know you just opened, but the next time they come in, they will expect perfection. If that is achieved, you will keep them as loyal and satisfied customers.

The movie and the restaurant industry are similar in the sense that they're both constantly reviewed and critiqued. This is good and bad. Like movie reviews, the reviewer will tell all their friends and family about the movie—the good and the bad. Restaurants work exactly the same way. A restaurant that struggles in the beginning did not prepare the employees for the opening day's onslaught of business. If the reviews are good, you are on your way to a successful and profitable restaurant. If the reviews are poor, you will have the chore of changing people's perception.

Each foodservice establishment is different—that's what makes restaurants so interesting. The skills of your cooks will be a major asset, but without proper training they will not be able to prepare the items on the menu in a way that reflects your intention. Any two cooks will prepare Veal Marsala in two different ways. In fact, there might be 20 different ways to prepare Veal Marsala. Each employee must receive the proper orientation and training so they can execute the recipe *your* way—perfect to your concept and vision.

Who does the training? Training is done by the owner, management, department heads and equipment providers. Sometimes the size of the operation will dictate the owner's involvement in training that is task-oriented. Before any training can take place, the owner or creator of the concept and vision must be fully confident that the key employees (department heads) are fully versed on the restaurant's concept and vision. You cannot expect them to train employees unless they completely understand the menu, service, and customer relations.

Your goal for every employee is the flawless execution of your concept and vision. If that is achieved, and you are happy with the physical aspects of the space, you will have fully realized your dream/plans. Five training sessions are needed to prepare for opening day:

❏ Session 1—Training for Key Personnel

❏ Session 2—General Information Orientation

❏ Session 3—Product Orientation

❏ Session 4—Hands-on Training

❏ Session 5—Pre-Opening Trial Run

The reason for writing this manual is to completely eliminate costly mistakes and fully prepare you for opening day. This section will describe the complexity and importance of proper training so you can determine the amount of time necessary for preparing your employees for opening day. If you can eliminate pre-opening mistakes, you will have a great chance of meeting all your critical timelines and be able to open successfully on any anticipated day. A vast majority of new restaurant owners, and even veterans, want to open the day after construction is complete, but this is an invitation for disaster. I have seen it happen too many times because the equipment, systems and staff have not had the time to be tested and cannot function properly. Before Session 4—Hands-on Training can begin, the construction workers need to be out of the restaurant, the inventory has to be delivered and stored, the equipment will have been tested so it runs properly, and the P.O.S. equipment and money handling systems have been declared fully functional. Only then are you, the owner and your staff fully prepared to start the hands-on training session.

Each restaurant or foodservice establishment will require a different length of time to properly prepare the employees for opening day. Training is costly, but it must be a part of your pre-opening budget. You must also realize and plan for the required length of time. It could be three days or two weeks, depending on the complexity of your establishment. At the beginning of this Instruction, I asked, "Can your restaurant get outstanding reviews from the time the first meal is served?" By now you should know the answer. It is a definite, "Yes." Allow the time it takes to train properly, don't skimp or rush, and you will have ongoing success from the first day you are open!

Training Sessions

Session 1—Key Personnel

In Instruction 11, I indicated how important it is to hire your key employees early. It is possible that most of your concept and vision is tied to a great chef who has a reputation for excellence. It is vital that each department head becomes an expert in the division for which they were hired. It is your job, first and foremost, to teach them to fully understand your concept and vision. They must also be well-versed in what is expected of their position. I highly suggest you schedule several round table discussions on operating and behavioral philosophies. Most, if not all, of your research and development will take place in those sessions. Menu items will be tested and perfected, P.O.S. systems will be selected, and strategies for employee training will be devised. This training phase will be sporadic and last for weeks or months. The main goal is to bring all your key employees to a full understanding of your restaurant's concept, vision and mission so they can train their staff and be able to answer, with authority, any question raised by an employee.

The menu must be tested and perfected until each department head is fully educated on each item. You will want your bartender to be just as educated as the waitstaff about menu items, their characteristics, and the appropriate beverage to compliment each item. I am not suggesting that you, the owner, have to know how to prepare Bouillabaisse—the key personnel/department heads will train the employees. But it is up to you to make sure your chef is in tune with your concept, vision and expectations. Once that is accomplished, they will be able to train their staff with full confidence. Again, this is an ongoing process from the date of conception to the hiring and training of non-key personnel, and as the owner, you will set the tone. Demonstrate and require expertise. Care about detail, character, respect and compassion from your department heads. This will trickle down to your employees and result in the ultimate experience for both employees and customers.

Session 2—General Information Orientation

This training session is both educational and motivational in nature, and everyone, from the owner to the dishwashers, must attend. It might last one day or take a few days, depending upon the size and complexity of your operation. This is your opportunity to have your staff fully understand your concept and vision. It can take place in the restaurant itself (if there is a clean space without interruption from construction workers) or in a separate building. It is important to have your department heads with you at the front of the room—this helps your staff identify the chain of command.

The following is a short list of topics to cover. You might want to introduce additional topics if the complexity of your restaurant warrants it.

- **Introduction**—Introduce yourself and your management staff. Tell everyone a little bit about yourself, and then introduce the department heads. Include each one's qualifications.

- **Mission Statement**—Describe in detail your vision and goals. Be passionate without being self-serving. Include your staff in your dream. They need to be as passionate as you are because they will have most of the customer contact. Get them excited about the concept, vision and the opportunity to work in a respectful environment.

- **Policies and Procedures**—Even though you introduced the Policy and Procedure Manual during the hiring process, you will want to spend some time on each topic therein. You don't want each employee interpreting the rules and regulations on their own. Describe your interpretation of each policy in detail so everyone understands the expectations for behavior. Rules and regulations are for everybody's safety. You will also want to protect yourself from litigation by making sure all reporting procedures are clear and in writing. Tackle this topic with passion and be sure everyone understands each policy and the procedure for reporting any unwelcome advances or incidents. Post all critical procedure information on a bulletin board to which every employee has access. Try to stay upbeat during this session—there are ways to make it fun and positive. Have a question and answer period, too.

- **Motivational Materials**—There are many audio/visual materials that have been designed for the restaurant industry. These are usually very good and can give the staff a visual of the atmosphere you would like to have. Using these resources is wonderful if you can truly "walk the walk." As an owner, you must be passionate, kind, respectful and approachable. Remember, employee attitude, whether good or bad, will trickle down to the customer. Create the ultimate *employee* experience and the customer experience will follow.

- **Socializing**—Have one or several social breaks with food and soft drinks during your training sessions. Get to know your employees. It is also important that each employee has an opportunity to get acquainted with the department heads.

Session 3—Product Orientation

Depending upon the complexity of your operation, you may require several product training sessions. The first should be in a large group. You want to educate the entire staff on the product that will be served, and your department heads will be vital in this process. It's always helpful to have completed the construction so the cooks can prepare meals for demonstration and tasting purposes. The waitstaff needs a full understanding of each item so they can answer questions posed by the customer. I highly suggest that you make available a written description of each product served, although this becomes a challenge if you have a large wine and liquor selection. Wine and liquor vendors will be glad to participate in training sessions and supply materials that describe their product. Product education is always a challenge, so find the best ways to teach your staff. Product knowledge is essential for a smooth opening.

Session 4—Hands-on Training

At this point, your restaurant must have been completed and fully tested. The health department will not allow food or beverage into the restaurant until the space is construction free. Training sessions will be conducted by department heads. Allow plenty of time—you want each employee to be completely confident in their ability to do their job well. The cooks must also be ready and able to perform under pressure. They may know how to make Chicken Marsala, but can they make that along with five other items and get everything plated to be served? Training is a big chore for every new restaurant, so make sure you have included it in the budget. You do not want an unprepared staff on opening day!

The Point of Sales System is a key component to a smooth opening. The company that sells the equipment will train the department heads first and then the staff. The P.O.S. representative most likely will want an X-amount of time allotted for training. Just make sure the system is running smoothly before opening day—P.O.S. system glitches are a major contributor to a chaotic start. Finally, spend time with each employee and offer them assurance when you see they are ready to represent your restaurant. And periodically get together as a group for questions and answers.

Session 5—Pre-Opening Trial Run

There are many ways to rehearse, but the best way is to invite a select and controlled group of employee family members to come in and have a meal at a scheduled time. Indicate on the invitation that this is a training session. The restaurant must be completely finished and decorated, and all management and staff should be in uniform and completely focused on the job at hand. Make sure the waitstaff does not serve their own family. The management should ask for constructive criticism from diners but should avoid lengthy conversations about problems. It should feel like you have opened for business. Focus on the positive. The purpose of this session is to work out the bugs.

There are many ways to train a staff, and several legendary authors have written books and materials on this subject. Do your due diligence and educate yourself. Do whatever it takes to have your staff ready for opening day! The better the training, the less employee turnover you will have, and that will save you the cost of more training. The better trained the new hires are for the opening day and beyond, the better for your bottom line. I believe you can open your first restaurant with very few glitches if your staff has been properly trained. The ultimate customer experience can be realized from the first meal served.

Training Sessions Checklist

Pre-Opening Training	Started	Finished
1. Key Personnel Training:		
Date:		
Date:		
Date:		
Date:		
2. General Information Orientation:		
Date:		
Date:		
Date:		
Date:		
3. Product Orientation:		
Date:		
Date:		
Date:		
Date:		
4. Hands-on Training:		
Date:		
Date:		
Date:		
Date:		
5. Pre-Opening Trial Runs:		
Date:		
Date:		
Date:		
Date:		
Other:		

Notes

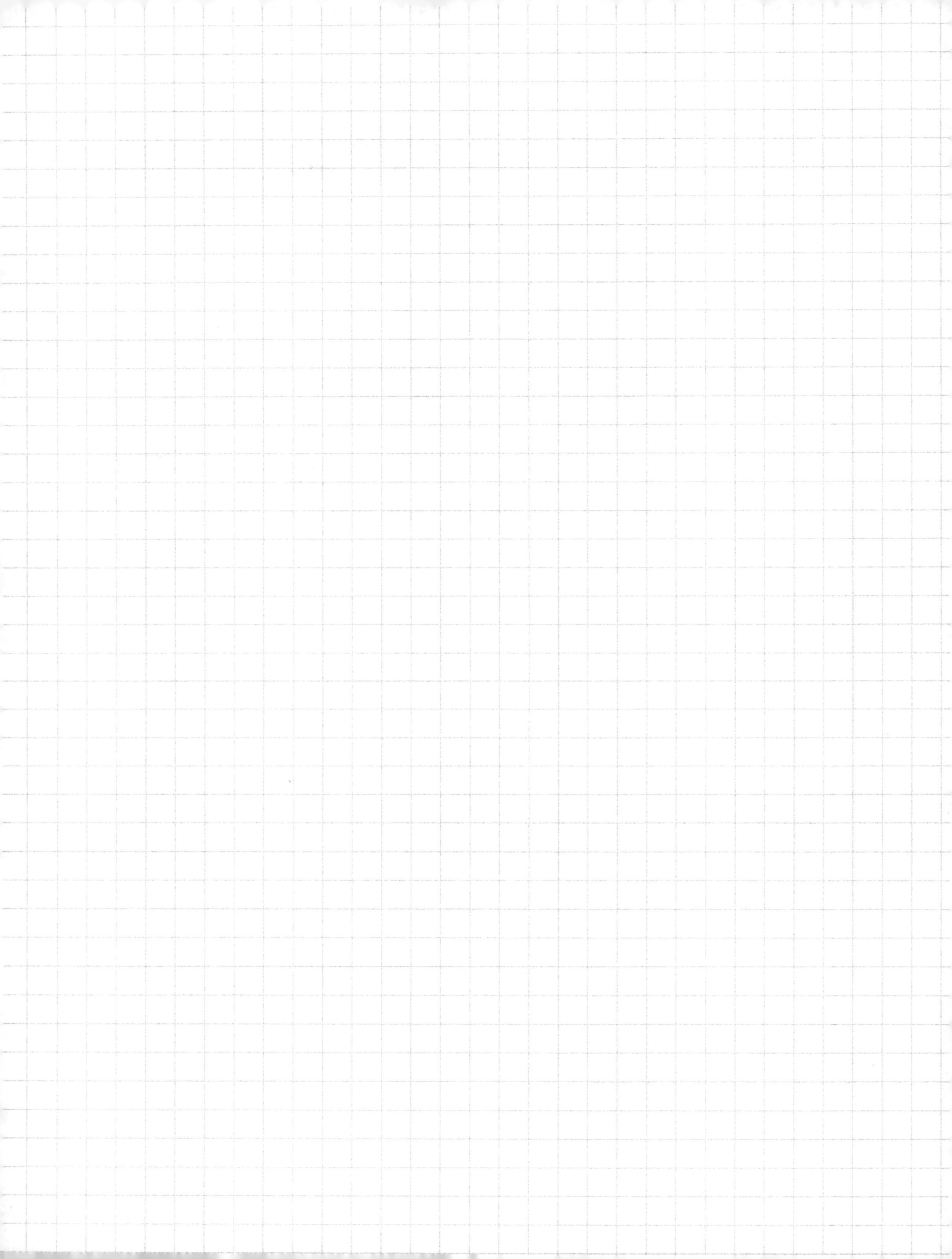

Instruction 13: *Grand Opening*

Instruction 13: *Grand Opening*

"Always bear in mind that your own resolution to succeed, is more important than any other one thing."

— Abraham Lincoln, letter to Isham Reavis, Nov. 5, 1855

There are many different ways restaurateurs celebrate their opening. The common way is to set a date and then do a promotional campaign. The owner runs ads a few weeks prior to opening in hopes of creating public anticipation. In most cases, this type of Grand Opening is nothing more than an announcement to say, "We are now open for business." Some limit their menu choices to a few specials to make it easier on the staff.

Don't be common! I would like to challenge each and every foodservice owner and manager to make the Grand Opening distinctively their own. You have followed each Instruction diligently up to this point, and this one is as important as the others. Grand Openings take a great deal of thought and preparation. You will want to open with such a bang that your customers will be clamoring for more. Many experienced restaurateurs will tell you to have a "soft opening" in advance of your Grand Opening so your staff has more time to become accustomed to the menu and service, but my experience with soft openings is that it's always a let-down to the staff's morale. The waitstaff is not busy enough to make money, and the rest of the employees are waiting for something to do. In most cases, a soft opening continues on for a few weeks prior to the Grand Opening. Realistically, it amounts to weeks of overstaffing, very little income, and possibly loss of employees.

Whether you start with a soft opening or not, your Grand Opening is your single most important opportunity to announce publicly that "the party is on." A Grand Opening is a public relations strategy that keeps your name persistently in the mind of your public. Press releases, news articles, newspaper ads, radio interviews and an introduction to your Web site are the usual methods of marketing an opening. Include menu samples, pictures, and your story on the business Web site. Raise anticipation! Get everyone excited!

Instruction 12 on Employee Training is crucial not only for the benefit of your customers at the Grand Opening party, but also for your staff. A stressful opening will absolutely deflate an unprepared staff. Take extra care beforehand so they are well-trained and prepared to handle an elaborate Grand Opening. When they make money, they will be energized and have a great time right along with the customers. People who attend a Grand Opening are typically generous with their tipping and very understanding of the special nature and challenges of this event. Train your staff well, and you will have a fun and profitable restaurant from day one.

Hopefully you have followed every Instruction thus far to perfection. You, your design team and staff have created the "Big Wow Factor" as we discussed. Now your Grand Opening should have the same "Big Wow Factor" as the rest of your space. Following is a list of some Grand Opening ideas that have worked for others. The main goal for a great Grand Opening is to achieve lasting success. Do what is best for yourself, your staff, the community, and most importantly, your customer.

Ideas to Consider for Your Grand Opening

Announcements

It is important that you publicize your Grand Opening date at least 60 to 90 days in advance so you can generate a great deal of public interest. The date will have to be set in stone. The space should be completely finished and the staff well-trained and ready by then. The only way to meet your date is with careful planning. Since this is actually an advertising and marketing campaign, be sure to include the following in your list of tasks:

- ❏ Periodically send out press releases and advertising materials.
- ❏ Get involved very early with local agencies such as the Chamber of Commerce.
- ❏ Arrange interviews with local newspapers and radio stations.
- ❏ Display signs and periodically change their message to invite interest.

Advertising opportunities are readily available to you if you are in a small city or town, and they will usually be very receptive to most of your marketing ideas. If your restaurant is in a large city, you will need to be a bit more creative with your efforts because of all the competition. Be aware of any codes or limitations on things like display signage. There are always advertising and marketing firms willing to assist you in varying degrees.

Private Grand Opening

You may choose to have both a private and a public Grand Opening. A private event is by invitation only.

Guests invited to the Private Grand Opening should include:

- ❑ Prominent city officials
- ❑ Local celebrities
- ❑ Investors and their families
- ❑ Local business owners that could be beneficial to your success
- ❑ Family members of your executive staff
- ❑ Owners and managers of all the companies that were involved in the pre-opening process
- ❑ The owners and staff of your design team
- ❑ Anyone else you choose to invite

This event is not a training opportunity for your staff—they must be well prepared in advance so you can make a great and lasting impression. You may choose to have cocktails and hors d'oeuvres or a full sit-down meal. This is considered a pre-opening expense. Make sure it is in your budget.

Consider including a dress-code on the invitation if it is conducive to your concept. Some type of entertainment might also be appropriate. As the owner, you should offer a short, prepared speech that conveys your gratitude to everyone involved and the excitement that comes with opening your new venue.

Public Grand Opening

This is a date you set well in advance. You are now open for business to the general public. You now have paying customers! You might decide to run a promotion special on the day of your Grand Opening, or maybe even for the first week. As much as you might want to impress your private guests, you will want the same for the general public because they will generate 90% of your income. Dazzle your customers with your food and service. Make it a point to visit them at their tables, and thank them for being a part of your Grand Opening. Make the occasion festive! Have live music if it fits your concept. Consider prizes, raffles and give-aways that will show your appreciation and entice customers to come again soon.

This is a real opportunity for you and your staff—they should be well trained to handle the onslaught. In fact, it might be best to be a bit overstaffed. Even if your waitstaff can handle a section of four or five tables each, you will want your staff to have a two or three table station during the Grand Opening. Add cooks if necessary. It might be a great idea to have an expediter who can help both the cooks and the waitstaff. You will want every guest at a table to get their food at the same time, and the expediter will be an asset in this regard.

Soft Opening

Most restaurateurs will have an opening that is not announced—a "soft opening." This can be helpful with an untrained or inexperienced staff. The downside is that you will be staffed to handle a big crowd, and if you are slow, it will cause a major letdown for your staff. No one can guarantee how many people will walk through your door on that first day. If you are on the main street of a business district, you will have had thousands of people witness your construction activity in anticipation of the opening date. You could have a line that goes out the door on your very first day. But if you are using a soft opening for training purposes, you will have a major catastrophe if you open to a full house. The question you should ask yourself is, "Do my customers deserve the best food, service and atmosphere?" In other words, never use your customers for training purposes. Remember, they are paying full price for their meal. Of course, it's your decision to make, but decide if a soft opening is really going to be beneficial for your staff. Or better yet, ask the bottom line question: "Will a soft opening be beneficial to my customer?"

Whatever you do, be well prepared for your opening day. Have a great and well-trained staff. Forego a soft opening if possible. Most importantly, make your Grand Opening the best customer and employee restaurant experience ever!

Notes

Summary

You have read the Due Diligence Instruction Manual, and can now make an educated and honest decision about whether or not you want to move forward with your venture. I know this Instruction Manual can come across as a bit daunting, but the truth is that doing your due diligence in preparation for opening a foodservice venue is hard work. Are you up to the task? There is a great line that I've always loved from a movie about a baseball player. Someone made a statement to him that to become great was really hard work, and his response was, "Yes, if it was easy, everyone could do it." What that quote means to me is that in order to achieve at a high level, you must work harder than others. Not everyone can do what it takes. If it were easy, everyone would do it. You might be qualified to run a restaurant, but are you qualified to open one? That was one of the first questions asked of you in this manual. This book gives you an opportunity to open your new and exciting venue with the highest likelihood of success.

Follow each Instruction diligently. Use this manual as a journal to keep notes, and then refer back to them. As far as additional resources available for some of the tasks at hand, there are great publications, articles, professional consultants and useful software programs that will help you fully understand the task and focus in on such things as financing, employee manuals, business plans, etc. Use whatever you can to further enhance the prospect of your new foodservice venue. I would love to give you specific Web sites to go to, but you will no doubt want to research just what you need for your own concept. Use the Resource page at the end of the book to record information you have found helpful so you can refer to it later. I have even suggested some search words to use. Beware of companies that want to sell you something you may not need. And if you'd like to contact me through my Web site at www.NationalRD.com, I'd be happy to give you some words of advice. I would love nothing more than to be even a small part of your success.

Each Instruction is designed to give you the information necessary for making thoughtful and sound decisions. Every piece of information you gather through each Instruction will confirm your readiness to move forward. As stated in each Instruction, do your due diligence with the utmost integrity. Follow each Instruction fully and you will save countless thousands of dollars. If during the process you discover that you are underfunded, my caution stands—do not move forward until you are fully funded.

This is an exciting time for us. You are about to realize your vision, and I am honored to have had the chance to help guide you. Your successful restaurant will not only be the result of your concept and vision, but it will prove your willingness to work very hard with due diligence. Act in good faith with the highest level of integrity, and you will confidently achieve the ultimate customer experience.

Instead of wishing you "Good Luck," I will say, "Here's to your due diligence!

—Frank Stocco

Online Resources

Instruction 1: Concept and Vision

Search Words: restaurant concept articles, restaurant concept and vision, secretary of state office (for available business names), restaurant trends, _____

_____

Web sites: www.ezinearticles.com, www.deloitte.com, www.foodandwine.com, _____

_____

Instruction 2: Business Plan

Search Words: SBA business plans, restaurant business plan software, business plan template, restaurant business plan articles, restaurant entrepreneurs, _____

_____

Web sites: www.sba.gov, _____

_____

Instruction 3: Financing

Search Words: partnership legal issues, restaurant funding articles, _____

_____

Web sites: www.sba.gov, www.restaurant.org/index.cfm, _____

_____

(Note: Beware of Internet lending companies! Not recommended.)

Instruction 4: Site Selection

Search Words: restaurant site selection criteria, commercial lease agreement articles, commercial lease negotiations, selecting a restaurant site, _____

_____

Web sites: www.about.com, _____

_____

Instruction 5: Key Personnel

Search Words: restaurant key personnel hiring, tips for hiring good restaurant employees, restaurant hiring, _____

_____

Websites: _____

_____

Instruction 6: Design Team

Search Words: restaurant design, restaurant kitchen designer, restaurant design consultant, restaurant layout, how to design a restaurant kitchen, commercial kitchen design, _____

Web sites: www.nationalrd.com (This is my design site. Feel free to contact me for a no-obligation consult). Visit three Web sites of restaurant architects that I have worked with to get a good idea of the "Big-Wow-Factor": www.shealink.com , www.ariainc.com, and www.bba-world.com. (The www.bba.com site has several articles on Buddy Guy's new restaurant, which I designed along with BBA), _____

Instruction 7: General Contracting

Search Words: selecting a commercial general contractor, _____

Web sites: _____

Instruction 8: Equipment Purchasing

Search Words: restaurant kitchen equipment, commercial restaurant equipment, restaurant systems, used restaurant equipment, wholesale restaurant equipment, _____

Web sites: _____

(Note: Use the bidding process as stated in the manual. Internet sites or equipment companies will want to sell you something that is not in your best interests).

Instruction 9: Miscellaneous Equipment

Search Words: restaurant POS systems, restaurant smallwares, foodservice equipment, _____

Web sites: _____

(Note: Use the bidding process addressed in the manual. Be aware that Internet sites or equipment companies may try to sell you something you don't need.)

Instruction 10: Policies and Procedures

Search Words: restaurant employee manuals, restaurant employee manual software, restaurant employee manual articles, _____

Web sites: _____

Instruction 11: Employee Hiring

Search Words: restaurant employee hiring, restaurant employee hiring articles, _____

_____

Web sites: _____

_____

Instruction 12: Employee Training

Search Words: restaurant employee training, restaurant motivational articles, fish motivational video, restaurant employee training articles, Culinary Institute of America training videos, ___

_____

Web sites: www.youtube.com/watch?v=r47xnTIhvdk, _____

_____

13: Grand Opening

Search Words: restaurant grand opening ideas, restaurant opening tips, opening day restaurant, _____

_____

Web sites: _____

_____

Other

Search Words: _____

_____
_____
_____
_____
_____
_____

Web sites: _____

_____
_____
_____
_____
_____
_____
_____
_____
_____
_____
_____

Notes

Notes

How to Open a Restaurant: Due Diligence

This is a guide for anyone who has visions of opening a foodservice facility whether a restaurant, bar, coffee shop, cafe, banquet facility, catering business, night club, carry-out, cafeteria, or any other concept. This book is designed to help you at the earliest stage of planning all the way to realizing your dream of owning and operating your own business. Follow the guide and execute the pre-opening tasks that are necessary before you ever sign a lease or buy a space.

Even if this is not your first business or experience in the foodservice industry, the information and instructions in this wookbook will build upon the foundation you already have. You can enjoy confidence in your abilities, concept and vision, business plan, investors, choice of location, staff, design team, equipment and vendors, and your plans for hiring and training all the way from the day of Grand Opening to your successful, ongoing reputation.

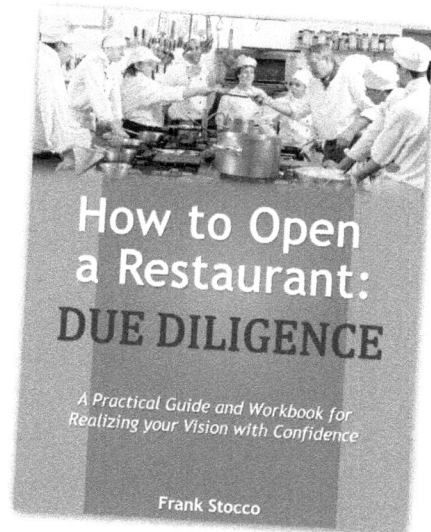

TO ORDER ADDITIONAL COPIES OF THIS BOOK (also available in spiral bound), visit Frank Stocco's Web site at www.FrankStocco.com.

THIS BOOK IS ALSO AVAILABLE THROUGH www.Lulu.com by typing into the search bar, "How To Open a Restaurant: Due Diligence"

TO ORDER QUANTITIES AT A DISCOUNT FOR EDUCATIONAL PURPOSES e-mail NRD Publishing at books@nationalrd.com.